# Artificial Intelligence and Machine Learning

*AI Superpowers and Human + Machine a Visionary Revolution in Finance, Medicine and Business. Find out Top Influent People of the Era with a Modern Approach*

*To all startups, students and people that wants to stay connected and updated.*

# Table of Content

# Introduction

Congratulations on purchasing *ARTIFICIAL INTELLIGENCE AND MACHINE LEARNING: AI Superpowers and Human + Machine A Visionary Revolution in Finance, Medicine and Business. Find Out 10 Most Influent People of the Era With A Modern Approach*, and thank you for doing so. With the rising world of big data, we are forced to develop effective strategies to help us make informed decisions. All professional fields have become very complex due to the growing demand to find the most efficient ways to extract value from the existing data. By downloading this book, you have taken the first step towards learning how to use big data and how artificial intelligence has made it possible to cope with the naturally outgrowing big data movement. The information that you find in the following chapters is very important as it will help you to learn how artificial intelligence is influencing human behavior and the possible impact in the future.

To that end, this book provides an in-depth overview of artificial intelligence and machine learning, highlighting their historical development and application in various fields including finance, business, and medicine. It covers how artificial intelligence interacts with human intelligence, including the possible partnerships between humans and machines and how each influences the other. People can utilize so much from artificial intelligence and machine learning to improve their lives and enhance their productivity. An interesting concept covered in this book is the AI superpowers across the world, and how they impact the development of AI today and possibly in the future. These include Amit Singhal of Uber, Andrew Ng of Baidu, Elon Musk of SpaceX, and Tesla, among others.

Although there as several options of Artificial Intelligence and Machine Learning books in the market, I am grateful that you considered this one! Please enjoy reading!

# Chapter 1: Understanding Artificial Intelligence

*"By far, the greatest danger of Artificial Intelligence is that people conclude too early that they understand it"*
*– Eliezer Yudkowsky*

It might not be possible to identify what part of the modern society that has not been affected or influenced by artificial intelligence (AI). Intelligence machines are influencing almost every facet of our lives including business operations and our daily activities with the aim of improving efficiencies. AI is so intertwined into everything we do that it is hard to imagine living without it.

AI is the major influencer of the 4th Industrial Revolution disruptive changes; the changes that will probably challenge human ideas. It is transforming the way we interact and live in an accelerating manner, making our cities to become smarter and help us manage our lives.

Despite the popularity of AI and machine learning, the purpose, and details of the two concepts are not well understood. In this chapter, we are going to discuss the key concepts of artificial intelligence and machine learning.

# Defining Artificial Intelligence and Machine Learning

As commonly defined, artificial intelligence is the ability of machines to make decisions and learn in a similar manner as humans. It is commonly known as a branch of computer science that deals with the simulation of behaviors of computer intelligence. Commonly abbreviated as AI, artificial intelligence refers to a computer system that can complete tasks that normally require the intelligence of humans, including recognition of speech, visual perception, decision-making, and language translations. This technology has influenced several consumer products and has promoted breakthroughs in physics and healthcare.

Machine learning is a sub-branch of artificial intelligence, i.e., all machine learning as components of AI, but not all AI count as the latter. It refers to the component of computer science whose aim is to build and leverage existing algorithms in order to establish generalized models that offer patterns and accurate predictions. Such algorithms are usually based on mathematical and statistical optimization. Suppose that your goal is to identify the patterns of a phenomenon using historical data; you may use machine learning algorithms to group the data and analyze the cluster results. With a bit of analysis, machine learning helps in the generation of automatic clusters or categories over time.

## History of AI and Machine Learning

Amidst the fact that artificial intelligence and machine learning have been around for centuries, their revelation was not possible until the late 1950s. A series of philosophers, scientists, and mathematicians attempted to explore the concept of AI, but it was not until the World War II when Alan Turing, a British Polymath, suggested to people how to use available information to make decisions and solve problems. Alan was able to figure out and understand the "Enigma" code that was used by the armed forces in Germany to securely send messages. Together with his team, Alan invented the Bombe machine, which helped in deciphering the messages. Turing concluded that a machine that was able to converse with humans could be referred to as an "intelligent" object.

In the early 1950s, John McCarthy, the top computer scientist in the US, organized a conference where the term, "Artificial Intelligence" was invented. Researchers across America became interested in understanding the concept of AI, thus, exploring the subject. Both Herbert Simon and Allen Newell were very instrumental in promoting the field of AI that would later transform the world.

In 1951, Ferranti Mark I, a unique machine, was able to use an algorithm successfully to analyze and master checkers. In turn, Simon and Newell invented an algorithm, commonly known as the General Problem Solver, to solve mathematical problems. Also, in the 1950s, John McCarthy developed the LISP programming language, which was considered a significant part of AI and machine learning. And in the 1960s, the development of algorithms was emphasized by several researchers to address mathematical problems. In the same decade, computer scientists discovered Machine Vision Learning which could be used in controlling robots, and in 1972 the first intelligent robot, WABOT-1, was established in Japan.

However, amidst the global effort to enhance AI applications, computer scientists realized that it was challenging to create intelligence in machines. In order for AI and machine learning to become successful, scientists needed an enormous amount of data. However, the computers that were available at the time were not well-developed to handle such magnitude of data. Corporations and governments lost faith in AI, and in the 1970s and 1990s, scientists experienced a shortage in the funding of AI research.

In the 90s, several giant companies once again developed an interest in developing AI. The government of Japan unveiled the plans to come up with the 5$^{th}$ generation computers in order to advance machine learning. The enthusiasts of AI believed that computers would soon carry conversations, interpret photos, translate languages and reason like humans. In 1997, the Deep Blue, IBM's computer, became the first to beat all computers in holding and interpreting information.

Over time, the exponential gains in the processing powers and storage ability of computers enabled companies to store vast quantities of data. And in the past 15 years, superpowers such as Google, Amazon, Baidu, and other companies have exploited AI and machine learning to a great commercial advantage.

# The Goals of AI

The key goals of AI include:

## Knowledge Representation and Reasoning

This is a field within AI that focuses on the implementation and designing of computer representations, which are able to process information. AI aims to automate these types of reasoning through the codification of relationships or rules in a way that can be interpreted easily by the computer system. Some of the common uses of knowledge representation and reasoning include a natural-language user interface that aids communication between computers and humans and computer-aided diagnosis that assists physicians to interpret medical records in the form of images.

## Automated Planning and Scheduling

This is another subcomponent of AI that deals with the production of automated action sequences that correspond to the measurements, which can be executed using AI systems. The goal of AI planning is to mechanize and automate the generation of any plan based on a set of actions as well as predetermined objectives and goals. One of the examples of AI planning is the self-correcting computer software, automated information gathering, robots that act as autonomous agents, and computerized suggestions.

## Natural Language Processing

Another significant goal of AI is the processing of natural language. This involves analysis and generation of language or data that humans can use for computer interfacing. The national language process aims to implement specific computer systems, which can process language data in large quantities. Some of the latest technologies that currently use natural language processing include the Siri app from Apple Company and Google Now.

## Computer Vision

The main aim of this AI component is to assess the automation and computerization of tasks that can be performed by human vision and system development in order to process, utilize, or interpret visual data. Computer vision utilizes several applications, including facial recognition, object recognition, automated image manipulation, and video tracking. Computer vision is commonly applied in facial recognition. Other applications are automated image manipulation, integration with virtual reality, object recognition, and video tracking.

## Robotics

Another significant goal of AI is robotics, which is about the construction, design, and operation of robots and machines that can replace human tasks. Robotics is a branch of engineering and science that includes electronic engineering, information engineering, computer science, and electronic engineering. Research on robotics is currently conducted to promote military, domestic, and commercial applications. Amazon, one of the largest global retailers, has autonomous robots in their warehouse with the role of keeping the warehouse organized and the operations more efficient.

## Artificial General Intelligence

The goal of AI is also to achieve artificial general intelligence, which demonstrates the system's ability to perform intellectual tasks, similar to human beings. AI achieves its AGI goal through integrated systems, including emotional intelligence, cognitive intelligence, and social intelligence.

# The Goals of Machine Learning

Machine learning is primarily used for the following output types:

## • Unsupervised Clustering

Clustering refers to the unsupervised technique used to discover the structure and composition of a particular data set. It involving clumping data into clusters in order to observe the resulting grouping. Each of the clusters can, thus, be categorized by a set of data points. The common algorithms used to address this goal include hierarchical clustering and K-means clustering.

## • Supervised Classification (Two-Class and Multi-Class)

Classification, on the other hand, involves placing data points into a pre-defined category or class. In some cases, classification problems assign a class to an observation or estimate the probability that specific observation falls under a particular class. An example of a two-class classification is giving a class of Ham or Ham to a particular email, in which 'ham' simply means 'not spam.' On the other hand, the multi-class classification simply means multiple classes. In the spam example, it could mean a third class, which is 'unknown.'

## • Regression Analysis: Univariate and Multivariate

as opposed to a discrete class, regression assigns a continuous response to an observed data. An example is predicting the price of Dow Jones Industrial Average on a particular day. The value could be a number, which would be perfect for regression. The algorithms used to achieve this goal are simple or multiple linear regression, forest or decision tree regression, artificial neural network, Poisson regression, ordinal regression, and nearest neighbor methods.

## • Detection of an Anomaly

Although we may assume that data is always sensible and well-behaved, this is never the case. Sometimes we get erroneous data points because of measurement errors or malfunctions. With machine learning, one can easily detect anomalies, which help in providing a measure of quality control. Common algorithms used to achieve these goals are principal component analysis (PCA or support vector machine.

## • Recommendation Systems/Engine

Recommendation engine refers to an information filtering system that is meant to make recommendations in different applications, including music, movies, restaurants, books, products, and articles. The common approaches used in the recommendation are collaborative and content-based filtering.

In order to effectively use big data, machine learning tools that are used to leverage different algorithms include:

- Data quality and management
- GUIs used to build models
- Model finding visualization and exploration of interactive data
- Comparisons of models to identify the best one
- Evaluation of automated ensemble model in order to identify the best values

# The Relationship Between AI and Machine Learning

Many times, researchers and students get confused in distinguishing between AI and machine learning and identifying the possible relationship. However, machine learning is particularly the study of computer algorithms, which improve with experience. The machine learning algorithms belong to a branch in computer science, commonly referred to as computational learning theory. AI, on the other hand, is a computer system divided into 3 categories: computational philosophy, computation psychology, and computer science.

Artificial intelligence (AI) began as a field in computer science, focusing its objective on solving tasks that people can do. It is approached using different ways, for instance, writing a program that implements standards devised for scientists. Although humans can do a similar task, hand-crafting standards can be a time consuming and laborious activity. AI has several tools that can be used to solve the diverse problems in computer science, including logic, control theory, search and optimization, neural networks, probabilistic methods, and classifiers and statistical learning strategies.

Machine learning is related to AI in that it is a subfield of AI. It is concerned with the establishment of algorithms, which are used by computers to automatically learn models using data.

Applications of machine learning are able to read texts and able to analyze the content. Machine learning can also listen to music, make a decision on whether someone is sad or happy, or find pieces of music that suit the mood of a person. Being part of AI, machine learning focuses on continuous data improvement, data mining, and task automation.

# Chapter 2: Artificial Intelligence Vs. Human Intelligence

*"It has become appallingly obvious that our technology has exceeded our humanity"*
*— Albert Einstein*

Artificial Intelligence and Automation are terms that are frequently used interchangeably. They are related to programming, or robots, and electronic machines that enable us to work more productively and successfully- regardless of whether it is an industrial vehicle assembly or sending a follow-up email.

In any case, it is more nuanced than that. Automation is fundamentally making hardware or software that can do things automatically- without human mediation. The term artificial intelligence was coined by John McCarthy as an engineering science of making smart machines. Computer-based intelligence is tied in with attempting to make machines or software mimic, and in the long run, supersede human behavior and intelligence.

The ideal situation which humankind is moving in the direction of presently is this: Automated machines gather data— AI systems "understand" it. We are looking at two altogether different frameworks that impeccably complement one another.

## Automation

Automated systems are the explanation banks record your installments in a matter of seconds, the reason why organizations send mass emails to their clients. It is what enables you to get your consignment shipped and delivered on the same day within hours of ordering.

Automation has a singular purpose: To give machines a chance to perform monotonous, repetitive activities or as specific individuals like to say, "to take the robot out a human." It saves time for individuals to concentrate on increasingly significant, innovative tasks that require human touch and judgment. The final product is an increasingly proficient, practical business, and a progressively productive workforce. A submissive advanced robot that never calls in sick or takes days off, and consistently takes care of business. It is no big surprise that organizations so readily adopt automation.

Automated machines are driven by the manual configuration such as work processes, programming edge case situations, and the like. Basically, a soldier machine that follows orders.

Automation will progressively affect the industrial revolution during the following couple of years. The effect of automation is already felt in particular businesses, and some nations are encountering the impacts more so than others.

The specialized possibilities for automation differ significantly across industries and activities. As automation innovations, for example, robotics and machine learning assume a tremendously incredible job in regular daily activities, their likely impact on the working environment has become a focal point of research and open concern. The conversation inclines toward a Manichean speculating game, which asks whether machines will succeed jobs or not.

While automation technology will dispose of few occupations in the following years, it will also influence parts of practically all employees to a higher or lower level, depending upon the sort of work they involve. Automation, presently progressing past standard manufacturing, has the likelihood, at least as to its technical feasibility, to change sectors, for example, medical and financial, which include a significant portion of information duties.

## Understanding Automation Potential

In talking about automated technology, we allude to the possibility that a given task could be automated by adapting current tested innovations. In other words, regardless of whether the automation of any device or activity is feasible, every occupation is comprised of different sorts of duties and tasks, each with fluctuating feasibility levels. Occupations in retailing, for instance, include activities like gathering or handling information, interacting, and relating with clients and setting up product display.

Technical feasibility is an essential prerequisite for automation; however, not a sole indicator of whether an activity may be automated. A subsequent factor to assess is the expense of creating and sending both the equipment and the product to be automated. The cost related supply-and-demand and labor elements speak to another ensuing factor: if perhaps laborers are many and mostly more affordable than automation, this eventuality could be a decisive contention against it. An additional factor to examine is the advantages past labor-cost exchange; including more elevated amounts of yield, higher quality, and fewer mistakes. Administrative or social issues, for example, the value of machines in a particular setting, should likewise be gauged. A robot may have the option to replace some activities of a medical physician, for instance. But for the time being, the prospect that this may actually occur could prove disagreeable for some patients, who are accustomed to expect human contact.

The likelihood for automation to sprout in an industry or occupation mirrors an inconspicuous exchange between said activities and interchanges among them.

Even when machines eventually assume control over several human duties in a certain occupation, it does not quite spell doom for the job in that profession. Despite what might be expected, other professions grow to fill the loss. In the United States, for instance, the massive large-scale distribution of standardized barcode scanners and related point-of-sale frameworks in the 1980s lowered the cost of labor per store by up to 4.8%and the cost of groceries by 1.2%. It additionally empowered various advancements, including increased promotions. In any case, cashiers were also required; indeed, their work demand grew at an average rate of 2 percent between 1980 and 2013.

# Partnership Between Machines and Humans

The greatest minds of this generation, Tesla's Elon Musk and Stephen Hawking, disapprove of artificial intelligence in a manner that certainly falls on the dystopian saying that "Robots and AI will have the option to show improvement over us, creating the greatest risk that we face as the human race."

Then we have robust AI advocates who propose that AI will support people but will not control or meddle with their lives. That is the general purpose of AI: To make advances that capably emulate what a human can say, think, and do, which generally would not be influenced by natural delicacy (people age and die).

Also, much the same as most people, that implies AI is terrible at mainly following orders. That is not what it is intended to do; it is meant to always look for patterns (like people), gain from experience (like people), and self-select the suitable reactions in the circumstances (like people).

In this way, AI is not a replica of me or you. It is tied in with making a system that is more powerful than we can envision.

What drives both automated systems and AI is something very similar that drives organizations: data. Businesses that are automated perform better and gain significant revenue growth. This, obviously, might be an aftermath of numerous variables, including the standard cross-segment of advantages related to automation. Expanded profitability; better business effectiveness, and most significant- representatives ready to concentrate on innovative or/and critical tasks.

We are not yet AI-ready. We are in the wake of cognitive automation. If we continue putting resources into smart automation by fueling it enormous measures of data, we can turn out to be significantly more powerful—as a people, and as organizations.

If we happen to imagine the world in the year 2030, the association among people and machines will reshape lives. Machines will supplement human abilities and help them accomplish more prominent efficiencies.

## Future Partnerships

Individuals have lived and worked intimately with technology, or machines, for a considerable length of time - from typewriters and PCs to the expansion of cell phones in our everyday lives. And, owing to massive advancements in software, big data, and processing power, we have entered a world with stunning new conceivable outcomes. We are going to observe an ocean change in our association with machines-portrayed by considerably more productivity, unity, and possibility than before.

As technology power increases 10x in five years, so will our dependence on technology, giving rise to a symbiotic relationship. People will bring abilities, for example, inventiveness and critical thinking, which can be applied against the foundation of human experience and cultural setting. And the machines will bring speed, automation, and radical new efficiencies. By training machines to improve their understanding of people, society, and organization, more of us will readily interact meaningfully with machines.

Profitability will increase, and new businesses and jobs will be made because of this new dynamic partnership. Machines will not replace us; instead, they will enable us to accomplish many more tasks.

## People as Digital Conductors

Human-machine joint effort empowers organizations to associate with representatives and clients in a novel, increasingly viable ways. AI assistants like Cortana, for instance, encourage correspondences between individuals or in the interest of individuals, for example, by recording a forum and sending a voice-searchable copy to the individuals who could not grace the meeting. Google and Amazon personal assistants can be integrated into homes, vehicles, and smartphones to do things like order products online, play music, book salon appointments, as well as offer customized fashion advice.

In 2030, we will depend on machines to oversee significantly more parts of our personal lives. We will successfully move toward becoming digital conductors. Technology will work as an expansion of ourselves, helping us better manage our day by day activities. With AI virtual assistants taking care of fundamental requests, human representatives can focus on tending to increasingly complicated issues, particularly those from troubled clients who may require extra support.

## Rethinking Business

The ramifications of this partnership stretch well past our personal lives and into how we manage businesses. The work environment will get a makeover as far as how it discovers ability, manages assets, delivers service, and facilitates careers.

By 2030, work will not be a particular place but a progression of tasks, which will be re-appropriated to the best talent the world over. Smart analytics, data visualization, and reputation engines will make people's attitudes and skills accessible, and organizations will seek the best talent and reduce personal bias.

In every way, regardless of whether it is finding the best talent, training employees, or calling upon an entire menu of services, deeper human-machine associations will be the power for change in 2030. We are approaching an era where every business will be a technology-based business controlled by software. Emerging technologies will reshape our lives and work forever.

## Learning On-The-Go

By 2030, the capacity to gain new information will be valued higher than the knowledge individuals currently have. Not only will employees have many jobs, but also the tasks and obligations of the occupations will be notably different from what they studied. They will gain the abilities and skills they require to execute their work effectively. They will routinely improvise, learn from one another, and make their way. These variables, combined, will genuinely challenge conventional organizations. Most will band together with machines to learn while 'on-the-gig.'

# Human Assisting Machines

People ought to assume three paramount roles. We should train machines to carry out specific tasks; explain the results of completed tasks, mainly if the outcomes are illogical or questionable; and maintain the accountable use of machines (by, for instance, keeping robots from hurting people).

## Train

Machine-learning algorithms must be instructed on how to execute the work they are intended to perform. Therefore, massive data sets on training are collected to show machine-interpretation applications to deal with everyday articulations, medical applications to identify disease, and engines built for recommendations to help financial decision-making. Additionally, AI frameworks must be tutored on how best to relate with people. Examples of these already exist like human coaches were expected to build up the characters of Amazon's Alexa not to mention Apple's Siri to guarantee that they precisely mirrored their organizations' brand lines. Siri, for instance, has only a dash of brazenness, as customers may anticipate from the tech giants, Apple.

Simulated intelligence aides are currently under training to show progressively subtle and complex human characteristics, for example, compassion.

# Explain

As AIs increasingly arrive at resolutions through opaque procedures (also known as the black-box problem), AIs require human specialists in the discipline to disclose their behavior patterns to non-expert users. These "explainers" are especially significant in proof-based businesses, for example, medicine and law, where a professional needs to see how a machine gauged contributions to, sentencing, or diagnosis, for example.

Explainers are likewise significant in helping insurance providers, and lawyers comprehend why a self-driving vehicle took steps that prompted an accident- or avoided one. Moreover, explainers are becoming a necessity in managed businesses- in any customer-front industry where an AI's output could be tested as unjust, illegal, or biased. As an example, the European Union's most recent General Data Protection Regulation (GDPR) presents customers with the privilege to get clarification for any design-based decision, for example, the service tax offered on a Mastercard or a home loan. Explaining one sector where AI will add to expanding employment. Experts gauge that organizations should make around 75,000 unique openings to cater to the GDPR stipulations.

## Sustain

Notwithstanding the people who can clarify AI results by explaining, organizations need "sustainers"- representatives who persistently work to guarantee that AI systems are operating appropriately, securely, and dependably.

AI can help our logical and executive capacities and elevate creativity. Take, for instance, a variety of specialists referred to as safety architects solely focus on preparing for, and preventing harm by AIs. The designers of industrial AIs that work together with individuals have given thorough consideration to guaranteeing that AIs recognize people and not cause them any harm. These specialists may likewise audit reports from explainers when AIs happen to cause harm, as when an autonomous vehicle is associated with a fatal collision.

Other sustainers ensure that machine frameworks maintain moral standards. If an AI framework for credit endorsement, for instance, is observed to discriminate against specific individuals, these ethic managers are in charge of investigating and undertaking the issue. Assuming a related role, data compliance officials attempt to guarantee that the collective data that is fueling AI systems agrees to the GDPR and similar consumer-protection guidelines.

A relevant data application job includes guaranteeing that AIs manage data mindfully. In the same way, as other tech companies, Apple uses AI to gather insights regarding clients while interacting with the organization's gadgets and operating system. The point is to enhance the client experience; however, unregulated data collection would likely compromise security, outrage clients, and cross paths with legal lines. The organization's "differential security group" attempts to ensure that as much as the AI is looking to gain as much as statistically possible, it is protecting individual clients.

## Machine Decision-Making

Through giving workers custom information and instruction, AI can enable them to arrive at better choices. Wiser decision-making can be particularly profitable for laborers, where making a better judgment call can profoundly affect the bottom line.

Consider how hardware support is being upgraded with the use of "digital twins"- virtual copies of real equipment. A company called General Electric builds the aforementioned programming models of its turbines and different mechanical items and regularly provides them with updates using the data collected from the equipment. Through gathering reports from many machines out in the field, General Electric has compiled an abundance of data on typical and deviant functionality. GE

Predix application, which employs AI calculations, would now be able to anticipate when a particular part of a particular machine may fail.

GE technology has, in a general sense, changed the intensive decision-making procedure of managing industrial equipment. Their application may, for instance, distinguish some surprising rotor mileage in a turbine, check the engine's operational history, report whether the damage has expanded in recent months, and caution that supposing nothing is done, the rotor will be expected to lose on average three-quarters of its useful life span. The framework would then be able to propose suitable moves, considering the equipment's present condition, the working environment, as well as amassed information about similar deterioration and fixes to different equipment. Alongside its suggestions, Predix can produce data about the expenses and money related advantages and give a certainty level of about 95% for the inferences applied in its investigation.

Without Predix, employees would rarely detect the rotor wear-and-tear on a standard maintenance check. It is conceivable that the damage would go undiscovered until the engine malfunctioned, bringing about an excessive closing. With Predix, technicians are cautioned to likely issues long before they manifest, and are provided the required data readily available to use sound judgment that can once in a while spare GE thousands of dollars.

# Fundamental Differences Between Human and Artificial Intelligence

## Feeling

Human intelligence is powerful because it is not constrained to objective reasoning. Different components of our cognizance empower us to manage the characteristic unpredictable and uncertainty of our general surroundings. They enable us to settle on choices based on shared qualities and inspirations that resonate collectively and empower us to know what is right without having to understand. Human intelligence enables emotions to influence their decisions and their conduct towards others.

A machine cannot do that, regardless of whether it needed to. Things become complicated when machines start making decisions that have significant outcomes, without the emotional setting and shared qualities that all people use when settling on such choices. Machine consciousness is unable to experience the feeling of pain, sweetness, agony, or even the emotions that music or colors elicit.

# Creativity

Putting aside whether human creativity is limited and, what exactly creativity is, it is unquestionably evident that artificial neural systems being grown today work out the rules as they come, instead of being taught. AlphaGo, the AI that crushed the Korean go grandmaster Lee Sedol, was fed a large number of games, however no rules. It worked out how to play go without anyone else's input.

In any case, can machines indeed be creative? Would they be able to be viewed as artists in their own right? If creativity characterizes being human, by what method can a collection of wires and transistors be considered to be imaginative? Maybe we are not as different as we might think. Our human minds are too constrained to even consider imagining how incredible machine imagination may become. Today's machines already display glimpses of creativity in art. There is software that generates convincing images of non-existent people by piecing together algorithms of facial structures.

# Machine Thinking to a Human Problem

At the point when there is no data, there is no AI. In that capacity, AI cannot solve what has not been collected in terms of data. Therefore, AI has a limit of knowledge.

Unless data has been fed to the AI system such as detecting emotions, heart rate, facial expressions, movement, routine, and the like, the system would not be able to understand human behavior. It will not adapt to different sets of motivations to which a human being is wired.

The unmistakable fixing in human knowledge will be viewed as the ability to incorporate informed and passionate speculation to make moral choices are adjusted to the unique circumstance. It uncertain that animals can coordinate, all in all, objective reasoning, and emotional deduction to make moral choices. Regardless of whether a few animals might do it, the suspicion here is that the sort of ethical quality rose would be extraordinary and reasonable for every species, and culture.

## Consciousness

By the age of four, children ordinarily start to get a handle on one of the essential standards in society: that their minds are different from other minds. They may have different convictions, wants, feelings, and goals.

Machine consciousness is another, mind-boggling and interdisciplinary research zone. It is firmly interlaced with AI, and even though it would be simpler attempting to disregard this point, it is a fundamental issue for everybody who needs to approach AI genuinely and from a foundational viewpoint.

Although there is immense interest in artificial intelligence, there has been significantly less interest in the collective consciousness. That is one motivation behind why we have additionally seen little improvement in how smartly our governing systems work- democracy system and governmental issues, business, and the economy. We are encompassed by organizations pressed with human intelligence that all things considered frequently show collective consciousness.

Even though there are no advancements in the area of machine awareness, or it is demonstrated that machine cognizance does not exist, it will add to the learning and systems of human consciousness. This will ideally prompt precious advancements in the fields of health, administration, and politics.

All analysts researching machine awareness will be faced with legal and moral questions and suggestions at some point or another. This can occur in different situations, similar to the animal protection movement has gone up against research and practice as a result of the acknowledgment of animal awareness.

## Uniqueness

The similarities and differences do not imply that AI is better than human intelligence, or the other way around. The point is, they are very different things.

Artificial intelligence is great at redundant tasks that have explicitly characterized limits and can be spoken to by data and awful at expansive errands that require instinct and decision making dependent on incomplete information. Interestingly, human knowledge is useful for settings where you need the presence of mind and conceptual choices and terrible at tasks that require substantial calculations and real-time data processing. Human intelligence and AI supplement one another, making up for one another's inadequacies. Together, they can perform undertakings that none of them could have done exclusively.

As AI gets better at performing an ever-increasing number of tasks, we as humans will find more opportunity to put our intelligence to genuine use, at being creative, being social, at literature, poetry, sports, and every one of the things that are important on the grounds that the human component and character that goes into them. Furthermore, we will utilize our expanded insight devices to improve those creations. The future will be one where artificial and human intelligence will build together, not apart.

# Chapter 3: The Technology Behind Human Machine Interface

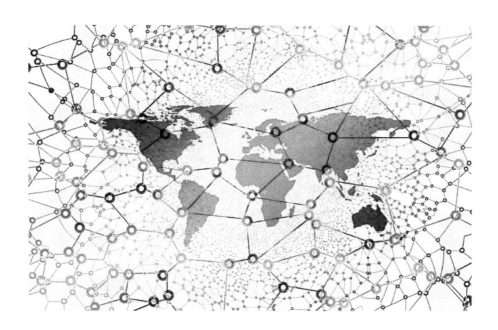

*"Technology is changing the way we interact as humans"*
*— Dan Brown*

In this chapter, we will cover the following:

- Definition of Human Machine Interface(HMI) and its uses.
- Styles of HMI.
- Anthropoid Machine Interface.
- Smart automation influence in lifestyle and relationship
- Hard and software.
- Configuration type.

- Market dynamics.

# Definition of Human Machine Interface (HMI)

The Human-Machine Interface (HMI) is a constituent of precise expedients that are skillful of controlling human-machine relationships. The engine boundary consists of hardware and software that will permit operator inputs to be converted as indications for machinery that will again give out the mandatory outcome to the operator. HMI expertise is being cast-off in countless productions like microelectronics, showbiz, and medicinal, military amongst others. It has helped in the integration of humans into multipart high-tech systems. The human-machine interface can also be referred to as man-machine interface (MMI), human-computer interface, or computer-human interface.

HMI has two interaction types, i.e., humanoid to engine and engine to humanoid. Being that HMI is ever-present, boundaries tangled can consist of wave radars, controls and marginal expedients, dialog acknowledgment, interaction info exchange using light, sound, high temperature, and other perceptive means that can be considered part of HMIs. HMI can also be used as an adapter for other technologies despite being considered as a standalone technological area. They are built based on humanoid bodily, behavioral, and psychological competences, which means that ergonomics will formulate ideologies behind HMIs. They can be responsible for matchless chances for submissions, wisdom, and restoration, apart from being able to enhance user experience and efficiency. Better HMI can give excellent and natural relations with exterior devices. The diagram below illustrates the HMI.

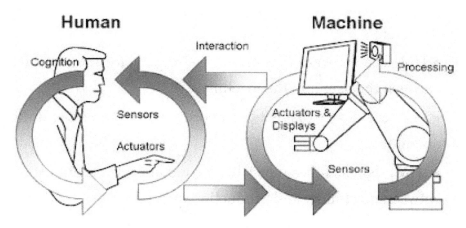

Figure 1: A HIM interface

There are advantages given by incorporating HMIs included in the inaccuracy discount, amplified scheme, and consumer effectiveness, upgraded consistency, and maintainability amplified consumer approval and consumer wellbeing, decrease in preparation and expertise necessities, bodily users, duty overload, amplified budget industrialized, and efficiency among others. Touchscreens and casing modifications can be referred to as samples of HMIs. Its knowledge is castoff largely in key and flat performances, array response, internet entrance, records involvement for microelectronics, and info synthesis. There are certified groups like GEIA and ISO provide standards and guidelines that can be applied for Human-machine interface technology.

# Uses of Human-Machine Interface

HMI system:

- HMI is a software that has been designed for the interface between the user and the machine.
- HMI is a device that acts as a border amid the PLC and the operator.
- HMI is used in industries to enhance communication between machinery and production plants.
- HMI will provide a graphics-based visualization of industry control and monitor its system providing real-time data procurement.

HMI Elements:

The elements consist of:

- Development of static screen.
- You are linking of dynamic.
- Trends
- Setting up alarms and securities.
- HMI and interactions amid PLC and HMI.

- Advantages of HMI

- It's easy to use for non-technical individuals.

- It's user-friendly.

- Recording of data.

- Enhanced productivity.

- Enhanced communication.

- Reduced costs.

- Easy management of the plant.

Human-machine interface goods feature the essential electronics to regulate and signal different types of automation apparatus in an industrial setting. HMI goods range from simple designs with standard LED indicator screens too much more multifaceted HMI systems with touch screens and many features. HMI systems must be vigorous and be capable of enduring the harsh environment. The HMI should be resilient to dust, water, and extreme temperatures and even at some point, harsh chemicals.

There are very many uses of installing HMI in your plant or facility as discussed below:

## Alarms

Plant operators can see signals that have been given by the human-machine interface to identify any malfunction of equipment and react quickly. Alarms help in preventing and alerting the operator before an emergency level is reached. Alarms can also help in tracking other problems and help in optimizing production processes increasing productivity.

## Reliable Messaging

As an operator, you can depend on HMI messaging for Facebook pages, faxes, and many more when there is a particular event. On other occasions. Operators can be alerted automatically when fuel levels of a machine are low, and there is a need to refill.

## Easier General Management of Plant

HMI technology will efficiently manage and execute recipes. It has high-quality graphics that provide a realistic view of the plant operation, giving the operator easy control from a central monitor.

## Testing Accurately with Simulation

Plant directors can check devices and equipment quickly by the use of a flexible HMI with simulation. You can achieve the testing from the comfort of your office without any equipment. This will help in reducing the starting time and enhance overall production.

## Reduction in Costs

HMI reduces operation costs by replacing hundreds of selectors, indicator lights, and push buttons among many others. Meaning it will reduce the addition of panels, cables, and consoles.

## Enhanced Communication

HMI enhances communication between various types of equipment throughout the facility with the use of remote, Ethernet, data highway plus, serial port, dynamic data exchange, and many more methods. You can note that having HMI can benefit your facility in operating, safety, and production. Industries like Red Lion gives a variety of HMI goods even for demanding industrial applications.

# Types Of Human-Machine Interface

There are different types of HMI, as discussed below:

## Automatic Replacer

It rationalizes the fabrication process by consolidating all the roles of each switch into one position. It replaces LEDs, on/off knobs, and buttons. Abolition of these motorized devices is probable because HMI can offer an optical design of all devices attainable on the LCD display while resounding out all the other tasks.

## Handling of Data

This kind of HMI is usually impeccable for applications that necessitate a persistent response from the scheme. They mostly come fitted out with substantial competence memoirs. You must certify that the HMI screen is enormous enough for diagrams, fabrication breakdown, and optical diagrams. It can comprise roles like guidelines, sorting of data, and fright management.

## Administrator

Chief HMI will be important in any presentation that involves SCADA. HMI will utmost, run windows and partake a lot of Ethernet ports.

## Selecting of Program Writing Software

At hand are three sets that you can pick out from:

## Trademarked Software

This is the software the builder makes available, benevolent it stress-free and permits it to have fast development.

## Hardware Self-Governing Software

This is third-party software that has been conventional to suite on numerous varieties of HMIs. It delivers the producer with liberty for HMI assortment.

## Vulnerable Software

This software permits the architect to have wide-ranging honesty in the strategy course and only be carefully chosen by a liberal computer operator.

# Human Machine Interface Applications

There are various solicitations of the human-machine interface:

- Convenience commerce can practice HMIs to notice water transmission and wastewater handling.

- They are used in the bottling process, where it assists in controlling all the features of the fabrication line like haste, fault alteration, and competence.

- HMI can control the cutting of metals and how faster it is done in metal manufacturing industries.

# Human-Machine Interface Advantages

- HMI reduces production costs.

- It improves efficiency and productivity.

- It saves on time, thus increasing profit margins.

- They can save data, which is convenient to be used far ahead for troubleshooting upcoming motorized hitches.

- HMI expedients have extraordinary innovation and capability to elaborate utilities than ever before. They can give high-tech urgencies like disregarding the need for a mouse and controls and talk of hardware to software.

# Human Machine Communication

In case you want to be useful, inspiring, and exciting, then you have to create a genuinely cognitive experience. Cognition is a mental process where you acquire knowledge and understanding through thinking, experience, and senses. Cognition will define how human process thoughts to interact with each other. In the case of computers, the perception will refer to a system that arouses human thought processes by the use of algorithmic models that are intended to augment human cognitive skills.

This raises an essential question like: how does the cognitive system arouse human processes? It is because it must activate your human senses; it must create a motivating experience and inspire your thought processes with the same goal of acquiring knowledge and shaping your understanding. This is known as *presence*. There are persuasive cognitive clarifications that create a presence in our lives through that presence, augment of your cognitive abilities.

Compared to non-cognitive systems, cognitive applications will go beyond what you experience today in transactional applications like pushing a button, getting a measured response. IBM can distinguish them as systems that can understand, reason, learn and interact as expected. To achieve this, cognitive systems will analyze vast quantities of data to constitute insightful, contextually aware, and continuously improve connection with users. Due to its growing knowledge of users' needs, goals and values allows them to deliver personalized replies, suggest relevant perceptions, and revealing contextually substantial discoveries.

For you to understand, reason, learn, and interact, there are various elements of human thinking and communication that cognitive systems should be able to recognize, understand, simulate, and analyze:

- Perception
- Motivation

- Learning
- Reasoning
- Knowledge

There are a lot of various levels of cognitive functions depending on the autonomy of the app. The low-level cognitive app requires a lot of support from the programmer, while the high-level app will behave more on its own. New applications might begin with low cognitive function because a user must train knowledge and behavior until the app answers reliably. With time it will develop more innovative cognitive functions. Every cognitive capability can have diverse levels of tasks depending on the quantity of user intervention.

An interaction amid the user and cognitive application might not need every one of these abilities, but the app itself will require the ability to finish a whole cognitive experience something which has a presence with the programmer. Human to machine interaction model ties the components necessary for cognitive systems collected into a methodology for creating cognitive skills. The main resolution is to direct and inspire intentional innovation and give structure for manufacturing responsible design decisions basing on human wants, expectations, and values.

# Part 1. Input: Understanding the World

## Knowledge

Man's impulse to communicate with technology; hammer, microwave, or quantum computer, will align right with the technology's ability to increase human lives to prolong your strength or reach. In the case of cognitive computing, enhancing that pulls you to interact with the ability to process vast amounts of data that augments your thinking. This will enable you to make the right decisions and bring about discoveries quickly than humanly possible. Due to this unique ability, it helps doctors spend less time to research and create more time to care for patients, creating target lessons for every student's individual wants, assisting industries in serving millions of buyers concurrently, individually, and proactively.

Knowledge can be termed as a summation of the whole thing a cognitive system recognizes from the ground —truth data that it's formerly educated with to learnings of every communication it experiences. Cognitive systems can be trained on any subject and are given a model for that area. They are usually better at reading, identifying, and remembering large amounts of unstructured info in ways impossible for the human brain to process. They can quickly analyze lots of pages of content and give a summary of highlights, or listen to many hours of music then create their songs revealing relationships and designs across formerly independent research. They will improve their capability to give you personalized answers, relevant insights, and discoveries with a new piece of data adding to their knowledge base.

Knowledge can be referred to as the applications ground truth and ever-expanding skill and expertise set:

**Good** – the form contains subject matter expert knowledge that sorts the application a competent tool for problem answering.

**Better** – the application will allow the programmer to update the knowledge base with trained data.

**Best** – the application will update its knowledge base by itself using live sources.

## Perception and Motivation

Responding to input from the outside world, cognitive applications will require to understand context, circumstances surrounding an event, statement, or an idea and this is because the system will fully understand the meaning of a programmer's intention at the moment of communication and give you insightful, timely, and natural answers. You will be able to recognize dates, author, and quality of information and validation of sources in regards to incoming articles allowing the cognitive system to tell what priority to offer to the new info. With a negative press regarding a company's good, the

CFO will want to start analyzing possible repercussions in stock charges immediately. A cognitive system can couple news alerts with significant insights and stock analysis, knowing it's an urgency for the CFO. The context will come from any source that will distress the system's capacity to offer intellectual answers to a programmer and can be deliberated from two perspectives that relate to the human thought process.

## Perception

If a cognitive system realizes that the user is at home and not in the car, it can conclude you are likely inquiring about your dog. Furthermore, if the system recognizes again that the vet recommended you take your dog outside every two hours due to the instructions sent to your mail. Perception is the application's capability to ingest, organize, and classify info about the programmers' physical and digital, recent, and historical context. Perceptual statistics are things such as location, time, date, expression, mood, environment, networks, nearby places, and connected applications. Perception uses APIs to stream information about the world where it includes weather, delays, social media, events, and traffic jams. When there is more data, a cognitive system can collect nearby awareness both historically, and at the moment, more insightful and natural responses can be.

The perception which is the application's capability to consume, classify, and organize information about the programmers' bodily and digital context:

- **Good** – the application will sort and organize information considering its pre-training.

- **Better** – the application is capable to categorize and organize recent information from live sources and what it has learned.

- **Best** – perception application will infer data basing on the other information, i.e., if Brian is in hospital and the doctors instruct him not to take fluids, the cognitive system will realize that he has a glass and he is drinking from it and can pass the info to the doctors that he is hydrated.

## Motivation

Accepting motivation will give the cognitive application the awareness about programmers' goals, values, and priorities so that it can modify an insightful answer that will meet the users' anticipations for communication with the system. There is data that will define a programmer's motivation and can be sought out by their setup experience, responses, expressions, preferences, and communications with time. With the growth of programmers' communication history, the understanding of the system of the users' wants, and behaviors also grow improving the knowledge with each communication.

Motivation allows the system to understand and prioritize behavioral and personal info about the programmer's reasoning to come up with a valuable response. This is done by evaluation of the success of previous reactions when the user was in the same circumstance that defined your wants and values at that moment i.e., a cognitive system can decide not to interject a call with a work notice because in the past the programmer lay off similar notice when on the phone with the mum. It can decide to alert a programmer to a news feed you aren't pledged to because the user currently is concentrating on this current topic at work. It can also listen in a meeting and resolve to send the team response on refining how to operate stand-ups in line with minutes of the meeting, considering the managers' goal to enhance responsive practices.

Cognitive systems are required to account for why a programmer is inquiring about a particular order. Consider knowing the expectations for communicating with a system that is built by an athletic clothing trademark against a system developed by a music review trademark. In case a programmer inquired every order on what to do on a Saturday night, you would expect a range of answers basing on the values the trademark of that system symbolizes. Cognitive systems have objectives and values that are demarcated by their inventors that need to be accounted for and conveyed in their reactions to meet the programmers' anticipation.

Take a situation where perception and motivation are the significant components for making a programmer feel understood. The system is expected to reflect ways that will the programmer is well informed of and can remember past interactions, anticipates wants without any directions. It should be able to reduce friction and cut the number of steps it will have to finish a task. If it's done in the right way, then the cognitive system will have a feeling that knows you and understand your wants.

Motivation, well known as the applications ability to understand the programmers' intention, priority, values, and goals:

• **Good** – the application is well conversant with demographic factors and trade focuses of its programmers and surface info for that reason.

• **Better** – the application can identify individuals and their personalized characteristics. It can be familiar with users' feelings and answer back with the most applicable emotion.

• **Best** – the application proactively communicates with the programmer basing on how you will answer back, i.e., an assistant is well conversant with the person to assist and plans on how to cater to their wants.

# Part 2. Output: Natural Response

## Reasoning

Applications mostly have intelligent communications with a programmer by easily giving the ground truth info that is stored in its knowledge base. By the use of its experience about the context of a user, the cognitive application will go beyond accurate translation and retort with a more treasured, big-picture answer. Reasoning can be referred to as the application's ability to have cognitive communications by considering all the info available through perception, knowledge, and motivation. If a solid knowledge base produces an intelligent response, it won't feel cognitive if the application doesn't serve the individual and consider your context in some way.

By having confidence scores to potential answers based on detailed findings and previous communications, the system can think about how to make up a comeback that is modified and foretelling. Single communications can have more abilities in use at the akin time, but the cognitive application will compose its response based on what it's studied to date, and aim at improving the answer in the future based on the programmers' reaction to that particular response. The reasoning is an application capable of having intellectual communications basing on contextual and historical knowledge of the programmer:


- **Good** – the app can generate predetermined responses that are precise to the domain or directed problem space. It necessarily doesn't use perception or motivation abilities when creating responses but relies on pre-trained knowledge.
- **Better** – it creates resourceful responses and relies on perception, motivation, and knowledge abilities when creating responses.
- **Best** – it will bring anticipation to the user's want, and respond directly to them creating recommendations that will have a benefit to your needs and context far much ahead anything stated explicitly.


## Learning

Where there is an interaction, cognitive applications will update their knowledge about a programmer, current data, and the world based on the programmers' response. There are situations where the user immediately hit off the link that was suggested without checking on the content. Cognitive systems usually update the way they interact with people basing on findings from personal and collective historical experience. They remember past communications and adjust responses based on those studies by enhancing adjustments to the confidence scoring of context in the matrix. Learning considered as the applications capability to interpret user responses and apply that knowledge to improving communications over time:

- **Good** – it will allow the programmer to train pre-packaged info in the interface. It doesn't teach the perception or motivation abilities and its purpose to create more trained knowledge.
- **Better** – application learns through programmer communication and behavior and explicit feedback. It trains perception and motivation abilities.
- **Best** – the application updates or trains its info without any user intervention.

# Smart Automation Influence In Lifestyle And Relationship

Previous years there have been major interruptions in commerce models. The maladies of the bygone are now megatrends for the forthcoming, and emerging technologies and digitization are guiding many of them. Many buyers have moved from purchasing goods to consume services, experience, trades having no choice but to change round their operative models fundamentally. You can achieve this by automation of supply chains. There are different ways to foresee this coming in practice above the following five years:

# 1. Robots Fitting Together the Industrial Sector

In built-up company's, robotics, and artificial intelligence (AI) will be approved in the next five years. It can be seen happening already, i.e., rather than having a contract out built-up to Asia, Zara fabricated 14 highly computerized productions in Spain having robots working by cutting and dyeing textiles thus permitting the commerce to embrace time-saving catalog tactic.

Customer markets experiencing rapid growth will want to increase production abilities. From 2013 china has been graded as the world's chief market for robotic technology. Upturn in the use of robots and AI can generate first-hand hope for countries like China that are trailing significance effectiveness in case of rapid rising factory bills and the increasing challenge of getting production workforces.

# 2. Massive Data and Analytics Will Be Castoff Across Resource Chains

Cost of sensors and microprocessors making production smart retain going down, motivating the comprehensive solicitation of engineering automation. Some industries cannot substantiate the worth of predictable systems, veil computing, and software as a provision, where software is centrally accommodated making it obtainable on a payment basis making the statistics organization and analytics easily manageable. Using big figures and analytics with the radar, robotics and AI technologies will together produce a smart end product.

## 3. Last-Mile Delivery Will Be Uberized

When it comes to distribution, companies are already working out on how to solve the last mile problem, i.e., people are allowed to edict from indigenous grocery online and refer a private purchaser to pick the kinds of stuff and supply. Other corporations are working on solutions like a Uber rush to get to the clients at the exact time. Others are at work on improving the superiority of facilities and broadening the structural analysis. In the near-term five years, a lot of similar ideas would be there to fit anyone's needs.

## 4. Expiration of the Great Street

If purchasers are not buying online, they can be over and done in the next five years. Attempt to deliver goods to buyers as customers faster, industries like the amazon will create more regional delivery centers. There is a Chinese who have invested in constructing its supply network. It has 82 storerooms with a total area of more than 1.3 million square meters in 34 municipalities across China with 1453 local delivery stations in 460 cities.

Not only trades that feel the waves, in the succeeding five years, but there will also be a renovation of the fund chain which will bring influence to people in countless substantial ways:

**Rising of Industrialist**—Above the past two eras, the growth of corporations such as eBay has conveyed up a fresh form of micro-entrepreneur. Most current scientific improvements will improve even additional methods for persons to earn a living, i.e., Etsy an online bazaar vending with arts and crafts that allow hobbyists ton to retail their merchandise globally. This shows that although supply chain automation modifications the world of toil, it will devise to offer countless current models of occupation.

**Putting Intelligence to Use**—Regardless of the high technical improvement, commercial is still considered to meet people face to face, interact, and build a relationship. The systematic transactional side of the vocation can be robotic and digitized; a lot of trade enlargement is all about devising first connections and offline management. New skills will, consequently, be well-thought-out to upturn associated to the heights they are at today.

# Hardware And Software

**Software:** it is a universal word castoff to define a gathering of CPU programs, processes, and credentials that implement some task on a CPU system. CPU systems will distribute the software organizations into three prime kinds: system software, package software, and solicitation software. It can be stereotypically automated with a user-friendly boundary that permits humans to interconnect more competently with a CPU system.

**Hardware:** It can be pronounced as a device like a hard drive that is obviously or bodily associated with a PC. Examples of a hard disk are CD-ROM, PC monitor, copier, and film card. A computer is bound not to function without hardware making it difficult for the software since it has nothing to operate. Both soft and hardware communicate with each other where software tells the hardware which duty it has to perform.

## Contents of Hardware and Software

- Software
- Firewalls
- Function
- Changes
- Interdependence
- References

## Type

Hardware is a physical device you can touch and see like a computer monitor and software programs can instruct the equipment to do a particular duty. Comparing the two, the software has no physical form. Both of them are associated with computers, and there are situations where software runs hardware like phones, GPS, medical equipment, and air traffic control system. Without software programs, machines would be considered useless, i.e., you can't communicate with the computer when it doesn't have a software operating system.

## Function

The software executes a specific task by handing out an ordered set of programmatic instructions to hardware. Hardware will serve as the delivery system for software clarifications.

## Interdependence

Hardware can't operate until the software is loaded and installed in the hardware to set the programs in action.

## Firewalls

They are available for hardware and software. Popular firewall choice is a software firewall that is installed on the computer and can be customized to suit a personals user security wants. They are usually found in broadband routers.

## Changes

It has been common to switch to new software or to use several kinds of software at a time; hardware is usually less changed. Software is created quickly, modified, deleted, but hardware needs a lot of skills and can be an expensive endeavor.

# Configuration Types

Besides exporting a single configuration object, other ways cover the needs as well.

### Extending Configuration Types

Extending an existing configuration type, you need to come up with a configuration file in your module, i.e., add an event viewer                                                                    you create, *app/code/{vendorname}/etc/events.xml* and declare a new viewer. You can find out that the configuration type is in existence in Magento, the loader and the functions authenticating schema by now present and functional.

## Creation of Configuration Types

For the creation of a new configuration type, you at least have to add the following:

- XML configuration files

- XSD validation schema

- A loader

To introduce an adapter for a new search service that enables extensions to configure its entities, then you have to create:

- Loader

- XSD schema

- Additional classes for your new type of work

- Appropriately named the configuration file

## Exporting Functions

You can find the need to disambiguate in your webpack.config.js amid development and manufacturing builds. You can export a function from your webpack config as an alternative to exporting an object. The function involves two arguments:

- Environment as the first parameter.

- An options map as the second parameter.

## Exporting Promise

Webpack can run the function exported by the configuration file and wait for a commitment to be reverted. It can be handy when you need asynchronously load configuration variables. As an alternative to exporting a single configuration function, you may export various configurations. All configurations are built.

# Market Dynamics

It is referred to as the factor which distresses the supply and demand of products in a market and is essential to economics as they are to practical business application. A lot of economists establish market dynamics. They have been considered to be the most developed in Porter's Five Forces of competition.

Market dynamics can also mean elements that affect the market. From the study of economics, they supply, demand, price, quantity, and other precise terms. From a trade standpoint, market dynamics are factors that affect business models involving the applying party. When compared, the dynamics may be the price of a barrel of crude, oil manufacturing, national stockpile, and more for oil firms.

For a sensible trade, market dynamics is incorporated in the market analysis of their business plan. These factors have affect trade so much that it would be neglected if you don't exclude them. Market dynamics play a vital role in the marketing plan of a business. They can play a critical role in various areas like the cost of products sold, distribution, logistics, and many more.

## Examples of the Market Dynamic

Beryl is writing a market plan for her new trade. She sees a real want in the fashion company for high-quality accessories like purses and necklaces. She will have a great experience in retail, giving her a strong base to refer back to. For her to finish her marketing plan, she has to complete competitive and industry analysis. She will have to assemble the market dynamics analysis for the fashion industry respecting accessories.

Beryl will also need to understand them to fill space for buyers not being served.

She will have to start with the company analysis. Looks at various statistics: buyer spending rate, retailing growth, fashion growth industry, brick growth, and mortar trade sales, and competencies of retailers. Beryl is collecting market dynamics to know whether the market can upkeep the business. She is sure whatever is done is a fundamental foundation for her hint.

Market dynamics come as a result of collective market resources and preferences. Due to this reason, market dynamics are unaffected by the actions of any individual or industry. Individuals act in response to market dynamics as an alternative to causing them. The market dynamics are active in health, organic, natural, and eco companies over their market LOHAS division. A founder of Mambo Sprouts Marketing Market Dynamic is a company leader in publicizing and promoting services reaching health consumers online at wholesale and by emails.

# Market Dynamic Services

- Market analysis and targeting publicizing

- Brand research and promotion of evaluation

- Demographic statistics analysis, census, and bureau of labor

- Marketing research, communal mapping and wants assessment(non-profit and trademark)

- Third-party industry/trademarked research and promotion amenities

- Marketing communication, direct mail, e-marketing, and PR

- Company leadership assessments

- Business marketing research and insights

- Communal partnership and local trade visibility

- Mobile trademark, advertising, and promotions

In financial marketplaces, some and not all, financial services specialists are knowledgeable about how markets work. These specialists make rational resolutions that are in the best interests of their customers basing on all the available info. Savvy specialists are basing on extensive analysis of extended knowledge, and proven methods. They work to sufficiently bring understanding to their clients' wants, goals, time horizons, and capability to withstand investment risks.

# Chapter 4: Artificial Intelligence Key Leading Players and Promising Startups

*"It's much harder these days as a start-up to do physical devices" — Marc Andreessen*

Artificial intelligence is moving forward very fast. It is now playing a critical role in your technological world across all industries, from Agriculture to Communication. From Google to Apple and Microsoft, every major tech company is dedicating a lot of resources to breakthroughs in artificial intelligence. Every company now knows you must-have Machine Learning in your story to stay competitive. Several private companies wield immense power and influence in the world of A.I. both in the U.S. and across the globe. Such companies are using the technology in a meaningful way, and they are succeeding in demonstrating real business potential from doing so. Here is a list of the big players which have power and resources to shape your future using artificial intelligence technology:

## Twitter

Twitter has invested a lot of resources to get into Artificial Intelligence Learning. The company has already acquired four artificial intelligence companies in quick succession. The most notable of this is the Magic Pony. The company acquired Magic Pony for a whopping $150 million. The A.I. company has developed Machine Learning approaches for visual processing on the web and mobile devices, and Twitter will use this to improve its systems for recommending specific tweets in your timeline in the near future.

## SenseTime

SenseTime artificial intelligence company already has big clients, including the Chinese government on its list. The company is supplying the Chinese government with face-recognizing technology to track her citizen. The technology has been lauded as the best, better than what Google and Facebook are doing when it comes to face recognition. Currently, SenseTime is concentrating its resources on developing autonomous driving technology.

# Qualcomm

Qualcomm is a chip manufacturing company that is committed to artificial intelligence. A.I. plays an essential role in 855 mobile platforms developed by the company. The chip uses a signal processor for AI speech, audio, and image function. Qualcomm Snapdragons powers some of your most popular smartphones in the market today. Keep a close eye on Qualcomm if you are a fan of the smartphone technology for new exciting AI smartphone features.

# Nvidia

Nvidia is perhaps one of the longest established AI companies and still plays a crucial role today. Nvidia's graphics are the be-all and end-all for machine learning and artificial intelligence. The company is active in Healthcare, higher education, retail, and robotics. The company is developing AI technologies that will be integrated into every level of vehicle manufacturing and autonomous driving.

# Microsoft

Microsoft is involved in Artificial intelligence on both the consumer and business side. Cortana, Microsoft's AI, digital assistant, is in direct competition with Amazon's Alexa, Siri, and Google's digital assistant.

The Artificial intelligence features use the company's Azure Cloud service to provide chatbots and machine learning to some of the biggest names in the business. Microsoft has also purchased several AI companies in 2018 alone.

## Intel

Intel has been on a shopping spree for several artificial intelligence companies. Intel has acquired Nervana and Movidius and several smaller A.I. startups in the recent past. Nervana enables companies to develop specific deep learning software while Movidius was founded to bring AI application devices with deficient performance. Intel has also partnered with Microsoft to provide AI Acceleration for the Bing search engine.

## IBM

The company has been active in AI ever since the 1950s. It is one of the pioneer companies of artificial intelligence and is still active up to date. With Watson, IBM has come up with a machine learning platform that can integrate artificial intelligence into business processes such as building a chatbot for customer support. IBM's clients include big companies like KPMG, Four Auditor and Brazil's bank, Bradesco.

## HiSilicon

HiSilicon is the manufacturer of Huawei's Kirin 980 chip which was unveiled at IFA 2018 in Berlin. Karin 980 has significantly enhanced the second generation of the world's first Artificial Intelligence smartphone chip. The chip can do things like face recognition, intelligence translation, and image segmentation at a very high speed. The chip has led to the development of many other smartphone chips by the competitors.

## Google

This is one of the largest and most important AI company. Over the years, Google has been acquiring several AI startups at crazy speeds. It has also created over 12 new artificial intelligence companies in the recent past. Google acquired DeepMind for a sum of $400 million. DeepMind is the board game playing champion.

The company is also funding the ongoing Tensor AI chip project for Machine Learning on the device. The company hopes to evolve from a mobile-first to an AI-first world in the computer industry.

## Facebook

Facebook has allocated immense resources in artificial intelligence, perhaps in recognition of how AI technology will play a critical role in the future world of business. Facebook's AI research group is known as FAIR, has been hard at work to advance the field of Machine Intelligence and in developing new technologies to provide people with better ways to communicate. The company also worked with two AIs known as Alice and Bob among others, but the project was terminated prematurely because of a technical malfunctioning that enables the couple to communicate in their secret language.

## DJI

This is perhaps one of the most famous Chinese artificial intelligence company. The company is currently valued at 15 billion dollars, with a 70 percent market share in the global drone market. The company has been increasingly entering the A.I. market with the latest drones using A.I. and image recognition to avoid crashing into objects while on the flight. The company is also looking at entering into the lucrative autonomous vehicles and robotics technological markets. DJI has also recently partnered with Microsoft for a drone to computer streaming project.

## Banjo

The company was started soon after the Boston Marathon bombings in 2013. The company uses AI to search social media to identify real-time events and situations that can be critical for emergency services and other organizations to operate faster and smarter. The company has attracted tremendous investment partners, including SoftBank, the Japanese telecommunication giant.

## Apple

Apple sees artificial intelligence has a critical part of its future. Consequently, the company has been busy acquiring A.I. startups in recent years. The company has developed products such as Siri and the company's newly Create ML Tool, which macOS and iOS developers to create efficient and straightforward training courses for their apps.

## Viz.ai

The company aims at reducing the number of stroke victims who don't receive the right treatment in time. Its software cross-references CT images of a patient's brain with its database of scans and can alert specialists in minutes to early signs of broad vessel occlusion strokes that may have otherwise been missed or may have taken too long to spot. The AI product from the company is already in use in some major hospitals in several countries such as Mount Sinai in New York and the Swedish Health System in Denver.

## Deep 6

The company has developed an AI product that helps pharmaceutical research teams to find the right cohort of patients to work with on their new technological trials. The company's software can pull data from electronic medical records to create patient graphs that allow researchers to filter for specific conditions and traits, leading to matches in short periods of time. The system's language understanding engine has been trained to infer some situations even if they are not mentioned in the notes. Currently, the company has more than 20 health systems and pharmaceutical clients in the states and across the globe.

## Armorblox

Armorblox launched into the cybersecurity market two years ago. It aims to protect customers from socially engineered attacks, like phishing emails which takes advantage of your missteps. It uses natural language processing which allows machines to learn and understand the language. Its software analyzes a customer's communication styles to get a sense context and then automatically flags possible phishing attempts, insider threats or accidental data disclosures.

## DefinedCrowd

DefinedCrowd taps human contributors to build bespoke datasets for clients. The company recruits freelancers through a platform called Neevo and assigns them tasks like labeling images or recording audios hastening their work with Machine Learning powers automation where possible. All the data created or checked by people get compiled into a format that customers can use to train their algorithms.

## May Mobility

May Mobility is taking on the self-driving challenge with a form factor that is more predictable than cars. They have developed autonomous shuttles. The company's software has powered shuttle services in Providence, Rhode Island and Columbus, Ohio where you can get a scenic tour of the city as a passenger aboard the self-driving shuttles.

# Artificial Intelligence Startup Companies Building Your Smarter Tomorrow

It is not only the big companies who are infusing their products and services with artificial intelligence. Other smaller companies are at work, developing their intelligence technology and services. And well, they are doing a remarkable job. Here is a list of intelligence startup companies you may not know today but which will define your tomorrow in a big way:

## Tempus

The company headquartered in Chicago, Illinois majorly focuses on health tech, biotech, and big data. Tempus uses A.I. to gather and analyze massive pools of medical and clinical data at scale. The company uses AI to provide precision medicine that personalizes and optimizes treatments to each individual's specific health needs. It relies on the patient's available data, such as genetic makeup and history to diagnose and treat.

Tempus is currently using AI to create breakthroughs in cancer research.

## DataRobot

The company is headquartered in Boston, Massachusetts. The company provides data scientists with a platform for building and deploying Machine Learning models. The software helps companies to solve challenges by finding the best predictive model for their data. The company's software is used in Healthcare, manufacturing, insurance, FinTech, and sports analytics.

## Narrative Science

The company is headquartered in Chicago, Illinois. Natural science creates Natural Language Generation (NLG) technology that can translate data into stories. By highlighting only, the most relevant and exciting information, businesses can make quicker decisions regardless of staff experience with data or analytics.

## Cognitive Scale

The company from Austin, Texas focuses on software and Cloud. Cognitive Scale builds augmented intelligence for the Healthcare, insurance, financial services, and digital commerce industries. Its technology helps businesses increase customer acquisition and engagement while improving processes like billing and claims. Cognitive Scale's products are used by big companies like JP Morgan, NBC, Chase, Macy's.

## AlphaSense

AlphaSense concentrates its model in FinTech. It is an AI-powered search engine designed to help investment firms, banks, and Fortune 500 companies find essential information within a large pool of scripts, filings, news, and research. The technology uses Artificial Intelligence to expand keyword searches for the relevant content.

## Clarifai

This software company headquarters in New York is an image recognition platform that helps users to organize, curate, filter, and search their popular media. The platform allows images and videos to be tagged, teaching the intelligent technology to learn which objects are to be displayed in a piece of media.

## Neurala

Neurala is developing 'The Neurala Brain' a deep learning neural network software that makes devices like cameras, phones, and drones smarter and easier to use. The company's product is currently used on more than a million devices across the globe. Big companies and organizations such as NASA, Motorola, Huawei are also suing this technology.

## NuTonomy

The company focuses on developing applications for the automotive and transportation industries. With a mission of providing safe and efficient driverless vehicles, the company is developing software that powers autonomous cars in cities around the world. The company uses AI to combine mapping, perception, motion, planning, control, and decision making into software designed to eliminate drive-error accidents.

## Sift Science

Sift Science provides multi fraud management services all in one platform. Sift uses thousands of data points from around the web to train in detecting fraud patterns. The technology helps payment processors, marketplaces, e-commerce stores, and even social networks to detect and prevent fraud. The company's product is used by leading companies such as Twitter, Airbnb, and Zillow.

## Zebra medical vision

The company has developed software for radiology and medical imaging which has enhanced the diagnostic abilities of radiologists while maximizing focus on patient care. Zebra works with millions of clinical records and images to create condition detecting algorithms. These algorithms will, in the end, help medical professionals identify high-risk patients' earliest and manage growing workloads with more accurate outcomes.

## Sherpa

Sherpa is a virtual personal assistant powered by predictive artificial intelligence. The VPA integrates with the user's entire web of devices, inferring and predicting their needs. Sherpa is continually learning and analyzing more than 100,000 parameters daily to keep the information updated and users organized.

## OpenAI

It is a non-profit research company with a mission to create safe artificial general intelligence (AGI). AGI aims at creating machines with general-purpose intelligence similar to human beings. With a focus on long term research and transparency, the company hopes to advance AGI safely and responsibly. The company has received sponsorship from big companies like Microsoft and Amazon.

## Tamr

The data management company was born out of an MIT research project to apply machine learning to clean and organize dirty data that is incomplete or inconsistent. Tamr's system automatically identifies sources of data across a company that can be useful together and tags in an employee to instruct the software on how to integrate it. The company has big clients using their software like Toyota, GSK, and GE.

## Bossa Nova Robotics

The startup has rolled out big slow-moving robots to 350 stores, including Walmart. The robots help keep the shelves well-stocked. Its systems read price labels for discrepancies and find gaps on shelves do it can alert management about the problems. The robots easily maneuver around the stores and interpret billions of images in a way that is accurate, timely, and reliably.

## Pymetrics

This online recruiting platform helps companies find the right employees by looking beyond experiences and sills on the resume. It has over 80 enterprise customers, including LinkedIn, Accenture, MasterCard, and Unilever. The companies use the software to have its top-performing employees complete a set of assessments as part of their evaluation.

Pymetrics gleans critical emotional and cognitive traits for different roles when job seekers apply to work at one of the companies and complete the challenges themselves. They are then paired with jobs that best fit their abilities.

Companies also use the platform for internal career development. It makes the process more efficient with better outcomes and increases diversity in a big way. The company is currently open-sourcing its algorithm auditing tool with the overall aim of preventing its systems from reinforcing gender or bias.

## K health

K health has developed a software that enables you to access medical services without having to step into any hospital the company's consumer app draws on a data set of more than 2 billion anonymized medical records sending subtle patterns in data to give users personalized health advice. The company has also partnered with an insurance company, Anthem to let members see how medical practitioners diagnose and treat people with similar symptoms for free. The software also enables you to have a live chat with the doctor but with a fee.

# Ways to Invest in Artificial Intelligence

Artificial intelligence is making serious inroads in the investment world. From funds to stocks to money managers, AI is infiltrating the investment landscape in ways no one had to imagine. What makes AI more attractive to potential investors is the fact that AI is touching almost all modern industries, including finance, national security, Healthcare, criminal justice, agriculture, transportation, and many more. Here are some good investment ideas that are highly recommended if you want to be part of the AI action in terms of investments:

## Invest in Low-Level AI Funds

There are a wide of AI exchange-traded funds for you to choose from. You can use management fees to help you pick a suitable fund for you. Pick a fund with low fees because this means that more of your money will go to investment rather than to management. Generally, one-year-old iShares Evolved U.S. Technology levies a 0.18% expense ratio and uses a proprietary algorithm to select technology shares. You can get a return of 23% from your investment in a year which is more double the 10.77% category average. For more AI options, iShares offers these low-fee funds: Evolved U.S. Consumer Staples ETF, iShares evolved discretionary spending ETF, iShares Evolved U.S. Financial ETF and iShares Evolved U.S. Media and Entertainment ETF.

## Invest in AI Top Stocks

If you prefer investing in stocks and you want to grow your A.I. stock portfolio, then consider investing from these firms:

- Micron Technology, a memory chip manufacturer which is likely to benefit from the demand for increased computing power.

- Nvidia corp.- this is another chip manufacturer with a bright future. The company has been trending lately and is expected to post positive results over the coming years.
- Baidu- this is a massive Chinese company which is investing heavily in AI With about 1.4 billion Chinese citizens, Baidu can capture a tremendous amount of machine learning data to both use and sell. The company promises good returns with the Chinese government deploying AI nationwide.

## Invest in Funds that Focus on Robotics

Stock picking is not easy. You may have a challenge picking the losers and winners. If you want to avoid this risk associated with stock picking, then invest in a fund. Investing in funds spreads the risks around. Robotics is a field of robots that are trained to perform as humans. It is a clear example of A.I. in practice. There is two popular robotics fund you can invest in: iShares Robotic and Artificial Intelligence ETF(IRBO) and ROBO Global Robotics and Automated Index ETF (ROBO). ROBO has returned 16.7% to date while IRBO returned19% this year.

## Invest in AI Customized Solutions

Big companies are now using AI to understand better and meet their customer needs. Such companies use big data and AI to understand and analyze shopping, browsing, and demographic data. This allows the company to market directly as well as advertise products and services that reflect the customer's shopping and browsing patterns. You can invest in such AI customized solutions to help improve the running of your business, for example, McDonald has embraced AI solution and technology with ordering kiosks and delivery services.

## Invest in AI Startups

Hundreds of new startups focusing on AI research have sprung up recently. While shares of these companies aren't publicly traded yet, you can still invest in them by using startup investment funds like Wefunder, SeedInvest, and 1000 Angels.

## Invest in Artificial Intelligence ETFs

More AI-based ETFs are being developed, but there are two ETFs which can help you get diversified exposure at the moment:

- Global X Robotics and Artificial Intelligence ETF (Stock sticker BOTZ)

- Nasdaq Artificial Intelligence and Robotics ETF (stock sticker ROBT)

# The Top Artificial Intelligence Stocks for Investment

There are a few companies at the lead working on getting artificial intelligence more involved with your lives. If you prefer to invest in stocks, then these companies are projected to offer handsome returns, in the long run. These companies include:

## Google Stock

The company has put incredible resources into many AI projects. Google AI is the company's research branch, and the company has wholly refocused from mobile technology to ai research as its core mission. The company as so far developed innovative AI products such as the Goggle Duplex a sophisticated AI capable of making appointments by telephone with perfectly mimicked human speech. Google is one of the leaders in AI development and is a favorite to investors seeking AI exposure.

## Nvidia stock

Nvidia stocks have been at the top of every investor's list of choices. Nvidia, the chipmakers from Santa Clara produces the most potent computer processors in the world. It has leveraged its unique technology in AI research. The company recently had an AI-based breakthrough in brain imaging through a partnership with the Mayo Clinic. Nvidia stock is expected to be on the rise in the coming days.

## Microsoft Stock

Microsoft Azure is the most robust AI platform which incorporated a wide range of tools so data can be collected and analyzed better. The new CEO has reinvigorated the company, and the market has responded well to the new changes with investors being rewarded well over the last years.

## Salesforce Stock

Salesforce is known for its obsessive focus on seeking growth and opportunities to scale. The customer relationship management software giant regularly acquires hot tech startups to improve its software offerings. In 2019 the company received Bonobo AI, affirm using automated analysis of customer phone calls, texts, and chats to deliver actionable insights. These technological advancements make Salesforce one of the new members on the list of best A.I. companies to invest in.

## Amazon.com Stock

The company has a valuation of $1trillion, and it is investing heavily in artificial intelligence. Amazon uses AI to power key capabilities like forecasting product demand, optimizing logistics and warehousing and improving the voice-powered Amazon Alexa virtual assistant. With about 360 AI jobs posted nationwide, the company is at the leading front in the A.I. world. Putting your money in the stock of this company guarantees you handsome returns.

# How to Create an AI Start-up

Artificial intelligence is all the new craze right now. If you are wondering how you can build your own AI startup, then here are some brief steps on how you can get started:

## Pick a Topic You Are Interested In

You need to select a topic of interest to you to stay motivated and involved in the learning process. Focus on an existing problem and look at the solution. If you are not successfully solving a problem that customers are willing to pay for, then your start up is going nowhere. Before you go far, test whether or not people are willing to pay for what you are planning to build.

## Play the Data Gathering/AI building a Game

Once you are assured of ready customers for your product, then build the first generation of your AI. You need to gather as much data as possible touching on your pet project, then curate it to make sure it is useful and then design a model and train it. You need to note that the process of data gathering, curating, and training is the most challenging part of your project. Training a model is very demanding and time-consuming. You will spend a bulk of your problem-solving efforts on gathering and understanding data.

## Build your Product

At this point, you should be having a working AI You need to improve your A.I. capabilities to make it user-friendly. This means you have to package your ai into a product which the market can respond to positively. Your product should have a user face with a range of capabilities. Your product must also be able to efficiently solve a problem it was created within a short time and in an affordable way.

## Develop a Means for Improving Your AI

Once you launch your new startup, you need to continue gathering more data that was not available for you when you were training your AI You then use this data to improve your A.I. to improve its accuracy. Determine the number of times you will train your AI in a given period.

Finally, in case you are having any trouble building your startup, consider enrolling in the online courses such as:

- **Learn with Google**-this is a project launched by Google to help you understand what A.I. is and how it works. It has a machine learning course for beginners such as GOOGLE's TensorFlow

- **Stanford University Machine Learning**- the course is available on Courser. The course can be offered for free, or you pay a fee if you want a certificate. The course will familiarize you with examples of A.I. driven technologies. You also learn the basics of software engineering

- **Nvidia-Fundamentals of Deep Learning for Computer Vision** -computer vision is a discipline that focuses on creating computers capable of analyzing the visual information as the human brain does. The course covers the necessary technical fundamentals along with practical applications of object classification and object recognition. You will also learn how to build your neural net application

# Global Human Machine Industry (HMI)

## What is HMI?

Human Machine Interface is a central control system that communicates operator inputs and receives real-time data and feedback from a PLC logic controller. An HMI provides an essential visual of what is going on inside a control system. It records crucial production information, including cycle count times and recipes for different processes. HMI has become the standard interface for operator control on new and upgraded plant equipment and process control system.

# HMI and the Global Market

The global HMI market is expected to generate revenues of more than $8billion by the year 2023. The increasing importance of safety, energy, better productivity, and sustainability will lead to the rapid expansion of the global human machine interface market. Moreover, the implementation of supervisory control and data acquisition (SCADA) and Programmable Logic Controllers (PLC) in factory automation systems will transform the market over the years. The global HMI market is driven by growing demand from semiconductor fabrication plants that requires control centers, clean rooms, and assembling plants for effective equipment control.

HMIs facilitate a high degree of customizations and are increasingly finding their application in equipment which is characterized by ruggedness and reliability in the human-machine interface market.

# HMI Market – Geography

The global HMI market is divided into North America, Asia Pacific, Europe, and the Rest of the World. Currently, this market is dominated by the region of North America. A rising GDP and recovery from economic slowdown are the main factors driving the North American HMI market. Other factors that make North America dominate the market include the growth in discrete industries, high adoption of advanced manufacturing practices, and increasing demand for advanced software solutions in manufacturing industries.

However, it is expected that Asia Pacific HMI market will witness the highest rate of growth owing to rapidly growing economies like India, South Korea, Indonesia, and China and the growth of automation in these regions.

The companies in the global HMI market are:

ABB Ltd., Advantech Company, Ltd Beijer Electronics, Inc. Honey Wall International, Mitsubishi Electric Corporation, Siemens AG, General Electric Co., Kontron AG, Ltd Rockwell Automation, Yokogawa Electric Corporation.

## Estimation of HMI Market

It is estimated that the Global Human Machine Interface Market will expand to US$5,579 million by 2019 as industrial efficiency takes center stage. The market is widely expected to grow at CAGR of 10.4% between 2013 and 2019 with the exception of topping the market with a value of US$5579 million by 2019.

The Global HMI market is also expected to further grow to us$8.96 billion by the year 2026, GROWING at a CAGR of 9.8%. The rising need for efficiency and monitoring in manufacturing plants and the evolution of industrial internet of things (IIOT) and the growing demand for smart automation solution are some of the key factors propelling market growth

# Future Technological Advances You Can Look Out For

The technological landscape is witnessing so many advancements nearing maturity. In a decade several of them will be accepted as part of your everyday life. They will influence how you live, work, and entertain yourself. Most will be promoted by business first before being taken by the wider society. While they will make life, easier some will bring fear and uncertainty at the loss of independence and control over your life. Here is a futuristic look at how the world is likely to change in the next decade with technology and innovations.

## Flying Taxis

Mobility is expected to change with the introduction of the on-demand flying taxis. An experiment in the area of flying taxis is being orchestrated by ride-sharing provider Uber Technologies as part of its Uber Elevate program. The company plans to deploy Uber Air-the electric aerial vehicles capable of vertical take-off and landing.

## Mobile Phone Advancement

A decade from now, mobile phones will have features that you usually see in movies. Such features include the hologram. In the next few years, hologram displays will be commonplace on smartphones.

Your phone will also evolve to become increasingly part of the internet and the Internet of Things (IoT). Future mobile and communication devices will be able to recognize mobile phones uniquely wherever they go shopping or take a pod to the nearest Hyperloop station.

## Drones

A future with drones in it is probably closer than you can imagine. There are a million experiments on drone use across the globe. Amazon is currently working on drones which will make deliveries. There are also companies working on drones that will make medicine delivery to remote hilly areas of the world.

## Creative Learning in Schools

From the infrastructural point of view, advances in technology will bring to bear many tools for teaching and learning. A good example is a virtual reality which brings alive various concepts, creating an immersive environment in the classroom. With the availability of cloud computing and storage, students will have access to their lessons and worksheets wherever place they are.

Teachers will have to reinvent their roles. They will become catalysts for problem-solving and for connecting students and the industry in the process of learning will become highly interactive.

## Medical Services

You will no longer have to go to the hospital for medical services. You can access these essential services right at your home. For example, portable versions of large scanning machines are being built by startups and medical technology companies. These new-generation devices make diagnostics available at home. Moreover, wearable devices that can monitor patients round the clock and upload data to the Cloud securely to the patients' health records are already a reality. They allow doctors to be alerted to a change in a patient's condition and help them determine the severity of the illness.

# Chapter 5: 10 Most Influential People And Their Contribution In AI Development

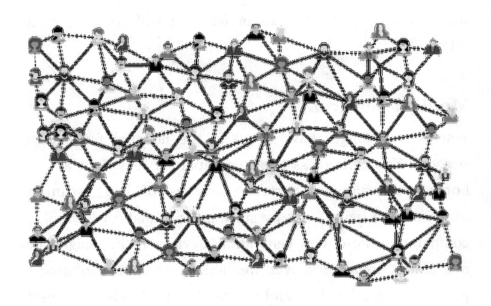

*"Technology is unlocking the innate compassion we have for our fellow human beings"*
*— Bill Gates*

As soon as something is working out, then there is no need to call it AI any longer. John McCarthy invented the word Artificial Intelligence in 1995 and ever since the AI Company primarily has undergone through various hard and soft moments. The moments have been accompanied by progression mixed with a lot of promises full of letdowns and disillusion. Coming up of enormous information, quick handling haste, and reasonably improved fever from the American Mafia, AI dignified to create a distraction on a gauge that can exceed the internet itself. As the world is preparing to witness a transformation of the AI companies, every individual associated with the modernization frugality will have to realize how AI will or will not bring impact on their company's daily lives.

# Part 1: Company Titans (Superpowers)

The following individuals have helped in shaping and enhancing the AI industry helping it to grow entirely into a thriving industry.

## Amit Singhal, Uber

Having been appointed as the new chairperson of the Uber's engineering squad, Amit is going to make a lot of changes to help improve the autonomous automobile breakthrough all over the Uber convoy.

## Andrew Ng, Baidu

He is one of the brains behind the creation of Google and now has been appointed as the chief scientist at Baidu," Google of China." Andrew is shaping the AI interaction in the two major economies across the world. There is no harm in him being the co-founder of Coursera, and he has 100K followers on his Twitter account.

## Elon Musk, SpaceX, and Tesla

He may not be a researcher of an AI company, but when Elon talks about the industry, a lot of people give him a listening ear. He is the chair of OpenAI. His recent announcement was the launching of a startup, Neuralink, which would create implants that connect the computer interface to the human brain through the use of AI. According to him, this technology would implant minuscule, flexible electrodes to the human brain via a neurosurgical robot.

## Jeff Dean, Google

He is the creator of MapReduce, Google Brain, TensorFlow, and Jeff has been considered as the heart of Google's most vital projects and has continued to create waves at the industry who first coined AI-first approach. Together with other Google employees, Dean recently announced the current ongoing AI projects that Google is working on, including Project Diva that assists people to command Google Assistant without using a voice, Live Relay, which is a speech-recognition app meant for the deaf, and project Euphonia, which is aimed to help individual with speech impairment communicate easily.

## Ginni Rometty, IBM

IBM ever since Ken Jennings 74 won on Jeopardy in 2004 has been working on Watson. IBM has positioned all its energy and future on Watson. Ginni also wanted to have Watson to tweet for her too. The jury has apprehended Watson but commended Ginni for turning the main focus of the 105-year industry on AI.

## Martin Ford

He is the author and creator of Rising of the Robots; he shapes the natural interaction around AI and robots. He is considered to come up with many bestselling books on AI and the future. His recent prediction, according to GE Reports, indicate that AI will destroy a lot of jobs compared to the number of new jobs that will be created. He noted that AI could threaten almost every job that is fundamentally routine in nature.

## Ray Kurzweil, Google

The main granddaddy of the association, Ray Kurzweil, has been giving out forecasts which are accurate about Computer Company for many years. He came up with the theory of Singularity, forecasting that in the coming decades we will get to a point where computing power will be so dominant that it will eclipse any reason human attempt process to process the speed of innovation.

## Sebastian Thrun, Udacity

He is one of the frontline brains on self-driving cars, Sebastian has also got time to start Udacity. There have been queries on why AI professors from Stanford began to a high online studying industry. This has been because they apprehended the disruption in AI that requires society to re-educate.

## Yann LeCun, Facebook

He is the leader of Facebook's group in New York. There is no further explanation about that. Reaching out about its inherent nature means that it will bring a positive impact on AI that will intimate a lot of people. Yann, who has a huge responsibility has come along with massive accountabilities.

# Part 2: Rising Stars

The rise of these people will have a significant role. Most of them are not that popular and will contribute positive energy in the coming decade.

## Boris Sofman, ANKI

Putting together the power of soft and hardware, ANKI is producing a high class of intellectual customer goods. It was first revealed at the 2010 Apple WWDC. ANKI has various hit goods that incorporate intricate intellect in human sociable robotic puppets.

## Bryan Johnson, Kernel

Many people know Bryan from his disbursement startup Braintree, his foray into AI is one of the most daring steps. He is ambitious and thus is the continent vast. They have been working to improve human capacity through direct assimilation using computer technology.

## Carol Reiley, Drive.ai

Carol is pushing ahead the autonomous driving uprising. He has been a long-time leader in robotics and is the wife of Andrew Ng. This is the first AI family in the United States to be precise.

## Charles Jolley, Ozlo

In case you need a friend then you have not to worry but get Ozlo. The industry has been training Ozlo to be a great and efficient assistant with each interaction and programmer and to create a useful part of your daily lives.

## Matt Zeiler, Clarifai

For there to be an interaction between AI and the real world, they need to see the world first. This is where Matt's company

Clarifai emanates in. The company helps in operating image and video recognition platform that many AI goods will put in use in years to come.

## Nikhil Budama, Remedy Medical

After graduating, Nikhil, together with his team, have been working to enhance healthcare for more accessible and manageable for every person and improving the focus and professionalism of doctors. Remedy Medical has been able to help doctors do administrative tasks and patients to have foster care.

## Rand Hindi, Snips

He is believed to be on the race of creating wise technology that disappears in the background and works. Together with all his team of stars at Snips, they are manufacturing artificial assistant that is no-frills and works.

## Riva Tez, Permutation Ventures

Riva has been known for being an AI investor and evangelist, bringing problems affecting healthcare and AI into the limelight conversations. After overcoming individual adversities, Riva is now working on changing both AI and the endeavor capital industry.

## Shivon Zilis, Bloomberg Beta

Being the curator of the market ecosystem, Shivon brought machine intelligence into the map. You can look for Shivon to influence the direction of the AI Company more so once receiving the support they want to improve in the coming years.

## Sinan Ozdemir, Kylie

Sinan was a former data professor at Johns Hopkins University and currently, the founder of Kylie, who is an AI that clones worker characteristics to automate interactions amid the industry and buyers. He is the editor of Principles of Data Science.

## Comet Labs Team

In a list of 10, it will be 11, and you can't miss recognizing this team from Comet Labs. They have focused on bringing AI and robotics industries to market, putting together the better of first stage fund boosted lab partnering with big corporations worldwide.

# Contributions

Below are some of the impacts on customer experience

## The Smart Spread

You have to think about what you in your pocket. Don't think about coins. This is because you are in your particular portal that every piece of humankind's knowledge was formed. Don't marvel at it anymore, but consider your smartphone miraculous. It's a digital helper that can answer questions, plan your life, and connect you to many resources worldwide right away. Don't think it's only your phone, but every technology is surrounding you is growing conveniently. There is a situation where your fridge can alert your milk level is running low; the kettle boils automatically when you wake up, cars dialing emergency services for you, have food by talking to smart speakers. You can have the AI toothbrush that will map your mouth and gives you a report. Nowadays everything has a connection, and the life we are living and the technology being used is that of sci-fi dreams. Just try thinking back how fast and perfect everything has grown comparing it to fifteen years back.

## Looking Back at the Past

Can you look back when the internet was readily accessible? Those are the days when you relied on CD-ROMS to get data, or you could go to the library. When phones had no maps, people would be stuck with an A-Z map to navigate. You might not be old enough to think about that, but you can still think about the hard moments of the slow net, tiresome rules on manual devices, and mobiles lacking Wi-Fi connection. You had to wait and be patient. Internet was opt-in and accessing it was to go through stressful processes installing a series of various technologies. Ever since the real-time revolution has been seen happening. This is precisely what it says on the tin, and it's the phenomenon of most things surrounding that is happening in the actual time.

## Real-time Revolution

It has made our individual lives simple and has changed the way we communicate with people around the world. With such an improvement, you have expectations of having information or data immediately. This is the first impact of AI on customer experience; there have been high anticipations from technology. You should anticipate your communications with technology to be effortless and anything not fast and giving poor usability sticks out like a sore thumb. When you are still paying attention, real-time revolution creeps in around you and changes your life.

# How Are Businesses Coping Up?

## Huge Gaps to Fill

Our individual lives are getting more comfortable. This has made it hard for businesses to excite you. You can have a slick, AI-driven breakthrough at home that you will expect slick, AI-driven advances in your communications with companies. It still doesn't mean enterprises are delivering and giving out their best. All of you will be frustrated like when websites fail to load correctly on mobile when they aren't receiving emails and slowly accessing customer service. It can be wrong to say that change isn't happening. Trades may seem not to be able to serve you as fast as Siri, but starting to be smart due to technology. What are some of the techniques that trademarks are using to keep up?

## Chatbots

There are chatbots, and at home, you also have Google assistant, and again when you get online, there are bots. Many businesses are getting chatbots into their websites, thus giving customer operation 24/7 and the whole year. You can look back at the days when you used to get your phone and speak to a business firm. Up to now, you can still find yourself in a FAQ section that takes a lot of time scanning. This may be a time you want to get a refund or update an email address. The addition of the chatbot has improved in ending the slow activities. They give you answers to your queries and are getting smarter in whatever assistance they are supposed to offer.

Chatbots are the best in replying to your FAQ and completing easy account tasks like creating new passwords. When you get the AI-powered chatbots that are being introduced to the market, then you will be advantaged. The new chatbot uses machine studying and natural language dispensation to understand what you mean and your mood sincerely. They can sustain humanized two-way interaction and help you with experience the same as what a real customer service operator offers. Faster and efficiently round the clock interaction has been a significant aspect of the impact of AI on customer familiarity.

## E-commerce Personalization

When you look beyond chatbots, websites are significantly getting smarter. Machine studying aiming at technologies are improving and pushing forward wise opportunities for personalized e-commerce understandings. Whenever you see adverts when you load a website, they are not personalized to you and based on other factors or things you like and don't like. Most of the retail websites will applaud goods based on the pages you have visited and viewed and the activities you had on the site. It's usual to see websites greet you by your name nowadays. In case the website doesn't recognize you by your name, it will be aware of your browsing site. There can be an offer basing on your location, or a pop up that will offer you a discount as a new visitor. You won't stop thinking about it, but it's more convenient than where websites were a few years back.

## Getting to Know

This is not the smartest stuff to be accessed online. You can see things such as WebVR where you can see, for example how pair of sunglasses look on your face before you decide on buying them. You can see 360 degrees websites that engage you within artistic settings and allow you to communicate with sections like video games. Biometric technology is also rising, and your iPhone cab is unlocked using your face. Trademarks are already attaching this technology for modernized checkouts. This has enhanced the use of fingerprints to finish a PayPal transaction. Soon you will be making transactions that will be verified using facial or voice identification. AI knows people better, thus improving and bringing about the changes seen online.

## Oil up Your Onboarding

It's not only browsing that gets more frictionless. Have you looked back about the last time you downloaded an app, digital good, or even a free software trial online? How long does it take to download? Guess you were downloading various pieces of stuff to make it run and did you experience consult instructions? All the tiresome onboarding experiences are things of the past. Trades are well informed that at home, customers are using technologies that don't need brains to activate in spite of authoritative abilities. This has brought about streamlining services offered that can help you run with a good in minutes. As long as you are running, you upgrade by a click or easily handle your account by the use of a secure self-service area. We forgot the days when you had to gather several different information or software to set up a digital good. Everything is coming back to the real-time revolution where people aren't patient at all. People are getting used to better and are expecting better from businesses.

# Impact of AI on Consumers

## Customer Service Costs

The impact of AI on the customer experience is not perfect. Weatherspoon has allowed customers to order and buys foodstuffs via applications, thus allowing you to sit down and wait patiently for a paid meal. It is easy and efficient; the experienced can be destroyed by a careless waiter that is delivering food to the table. Technology can increase the speed and transactional of tasks, and there is no doubt about it at all. But again, there is an amount of technology that can save your industry from poor customer services. AI can take that risk and break or make your experience. Technology has been considered tremendous, but many businesses can't afford to robotize their workers. You may be in love with slick skills, but customers still want a friendly human feeling.

## Rivals or Bros?

You must get to understand why there is love for a human feeling or touch. Machines are wise, but still, they don't follow us as humans do. There is some barrier. There can be jokes shared between you and the robot, but you can share a smile. AI won't be able to access your sarcastic tone or your dry sense of humor. Robotic receptionist won't understand what your raised eyebrows mean, and chatbot won't realize what wow represent. Businesses relying on AI have a risk of alienating their buyers and enhancing horrible robotic experiences. Think of a situation where you are frustrated and want someone to talk to, will you choose a sympathetic human or machine?

## Not All Doom and Gloom

There is an open place for AI when it's used subtly to assist service unlike overpower it. Using it well it will impact AI on customer experience, thus being relaxed and productive. AI has pushed us to work all round the clock service. You can visit a company website at any time of the night and ask a question through their bot and have an answer immediately. You will realize that you aren't talking to a human, but still, it won't matter. You can't expect to speak to an operator at midnight you will be happy to have been helped at that time of the night.

AI is a big boost for shopping online. North Face is an example of a company that has improved their operations using AI. North Face is assisting online buyers in getting their perfect goods. The use of voice input technology questions buyers and when they want to have their rights. This creates a great experience.

## Offline AI

Everything is not about online because AI will assist you to get better services in physical stores. You have to consider geolocation. You have to know where and who allows trades to send you real-time. If you a fan of coffee and it's just around you then there will be an advantage to have an offer enticing you to have your favorite cappuccino. AI has an interest in how humans look. Technology has adjusted adverts depending on time and date. This has brought about great bespoke advertising experience for every individual. Facial recognition has now been captured. You can start seeing offers on your computer screens basing on in-store dwell time.

## Fine Balance

This is an example of AI being used as a refreshing addition to streamlining the customer journey. When you are used to this, then the AI influence on customer experience will be impressive and wise.

# Impact of AI on Companies

## Automation Anxiety

You have seen how AI has an impact on the customer; you can also ask about its effect on the industry testing its implementation. You can be naïve if you claim AI will be leeway and daisies for industries straight away. There has been a series of hindrances to pass through before AI comes up with universal joy in the office. You to put into consideration that the world is getting into automation anxiety, and it causes fear. AI has come up with increasingly sophisticated and affordable developments that humans can replace. Everyone is worried that robots and automated processes will take away jobs from people. This should not be a surprise because AI is taking over even white-collar jobs in marketing nowadays. The tasks robots can perform are enlarging. In the offices, a lot of complicated techniques are being enabled, thus the creation of software that can work automatically executing difficult tasks. With the quick development of AI, then most humans tend to find their jobs at risk.

## Morale Dive

It will give a morale challenge to industries that want to introduce AI. Bosses are required to think about effects that could be there when introducing AI on their team. Workers can start panicking and fear the loss of their job. They can begin interacting with others and spread rumors all over the office. It can result in many workers starting to look for other places to work. Implementation of AI could mean traders see workers' morale take a nosedive, and can bring a negative effect on productivity. This is something that most bosses don't consider. C-suite is eventually focused on metrics, and their bonuses are tied to money increasing.

## All Change

Coming up with AI in the workplace has brought about a significant shift in the way workplace leadership is conducted. How can human and AI partners together in an integrated office? An increase in the need for workplace leadership training has focused on AI. Bosses are supposed to manage their environs populated by robots and humans effectively; thus, not an easy task to lead such a place. There must be skills that have to be upgraded to bring change. A lot of enhancements are being automated, thus the evolution of jobs. Trades have been busy trying to prepare workplaces for AI.

## Trust Matters

The impact of AI on customer experience can bring risk to the trademark. How can AI not be doubted to work the same as a human? When you have an automated function, there will no humanity skills like empathy, emotions, negotiation, and crisis solutions. This can bring about a problem for AI used in the customer context. You must have a requirement that maintains the capability to talk to a human agent and not robots. Some queries may want an agent to think deeply and have empathy for a buyer. You cannot fully trust AI considering this. Company operations may not be ready for AI, and AI may not be prepared too for the integration of company operations. When you handled AI implementations in the wrong way, then you could be in for a negative effect on the company's operations worse than they were. This can disgruntle buyers and reduce the morale of employees.

## Flipside

This can be one side of the coin, and risks are coming with AI, and at the same time, some rewards will be gained or incorporated. You will make a big step by saving money by bringing in AI. This is because it has enhanced efficiency and helped industries to manage time, resources, and energy. AI systems can hold up lots of work of workers helping you faster and having informed decisions. AI also comes with some intelligence that corrects human mistakes and has predictive minds i.e., can discuss and tell the number of business intelligence. This can help in enhancing your experience and gives you room to improve your interactions with customers. This shows that AI can assist in making buyers happy and optimize your forthcoming chances. You should also consider the competitive side of it. AI has still not developed that much, and when you start to deploy it, then there are chances of being the future leader. You should be wise enough to make use of technology trends and be an expert in the developing area. Don't consider it to be a negative impact on human workers. From the other side, AI could come up with better levels of jobs and put out the tiresome administrator that comes along the way of production.

# A View Of The Future

## Physical-World

You can't easily explain how AI will develop, but a lot of experts have seen some sense when tasks start increasing, thus making it easy for a computer to process. In the coming ten years, AI will be able to take over difficult jobs and time-wasting tasks that humans do every day. The impact of AI will rely mostly on cyborgs. Robotics operations are like to increase. In the ordinary world, you can imagine AI in stores that can choose the music to play based on the needs of the customers. AI can also decide wallpaper, artwork that a crowd prefers.

## Digital World

Not only will the physical spaces be smart. There are services such as Siri; Google Assistant will continue being active and very soon will be genuine to assist whenever you want whatever the topic. Complex mind blogging prediction, a lot of people will disagree that AI will conquer digital tech out of a 2D screen-imprison plan. Your main programmer interface can become the physical environment surrounding you. Looking at history, you can rely on 2D displays to have a game or communicate with a website i.e., you can see AI and internet advancing; thus, this can be replaced by the environment. You can as well have full-scale school field trips being done in a classroom using the VR-kits, boardrooms where performances show three dimension experience that can be felt. Nobody can tell if the virtual world will end up being better than the real world.

## Power of Thinking

When you look beyond, you can see we are getting to a point where AI needs no interface whatsoever. Early this year, you saw Mark Zuckerberg announced that Facebook is working on a direct mind interface that will let you navigate technology just from thought. He is not the only one working on mind interfaces. Elon Musk is creating a brain-machine interface that can connect humans to a computer without any hurdle of input mechanisms. Input has been considered to be a significant blocker, and there have been thoughts that interfaces would break many bottlenecks like has never been seen before. Employees in the offices will one day have to control machines with their minds by sending a thought to an AI system. AI is going to be everywhere, invisible but accessible from our minds.

# Chapter 6: AI Applications: The Impact of AI in Finance, Medicine, and Business

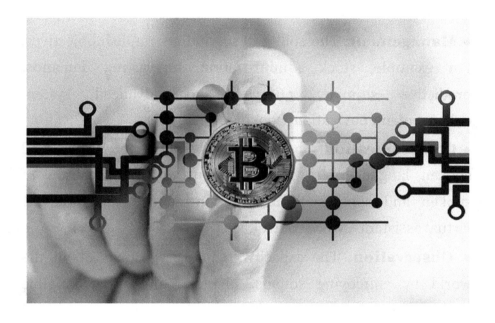

*"Mining asteroids will ultimately benefit humanity on and off the Earth in a multitude of ways"*
*— Peter Diamandis*

Artificial Intelligence or Augmented Intelligence is significant because it can help tackle primarily troublesome issues in different sectors, for example, manufacturing, retail, medicine, entertainment, transport, and utilities. Artificial intelligence applications can be gathered into these classes:

- **Data**: The capacity to exhibit information about the world. For example, financial management, asset trading forecast, legal assessment, gaming, and autonomous weapons systems.

- **Reason**: The capacity to tackle issues through logical derivation. For example, advertising, marketing, and predictive analysis.

- **Management**: The ability to set and accomplish objectives. For example, stock administration, forecasting demands, predictive support, physical and advanced system enhancement, navigation, booking, logistics.

- **Communication**: The capacity to comprehend written and spoken language. For example, constant interpretation of spoken and composed dialects, continuous translation, AI virtual assistants, voice control.

- **Observation**: The capacity to interpret things about the world by employing sounds, pictures, and other tangible information sources. Examples of this feature are medical diagnosis and treatment, self-driven vehicles, surveillance.

# AI in Business

Artificial Intelligence is reasonably the resurrection of computer code. It is a variety of computer code that formulates decisions on its own, that can act even in unforeseen events by the programmers. As opposed to traditional software, AI features a broader latitude of decision-making ability. Those traits build Artificial Intelligence into a precious asset throughout several industries; be it to assist guests and employees develop their approach around a company premises expeditiously, or carrying out a task as complicated as monitoring a turbine to predict its next repairs.

Machine learning is employed usually in systems that capture large amounts of data. As an example, smart energy management systems collect data from sensors mounted to different assets. Machine learning algorithms then contextualize the data troves and hand them over to human decision-makers to higher perceive the use of energy and demands of maintenance.

Many businesses take up computer science (AI) technology to undertake cut back of operational prices, increase efficacy, grow revenue, and improve client experience.

## Artificial Intelligence Impact on Business

By deploying proper AI technology, your business could gain the capability to:

1. Save time and cash by automating and optimizing routine processes and tasks.

## 2. Increase productivity and functional efficiencies

The automation potential offered by AI to today's business activities and functions has gone farther than the assembly lines in history. In many business functions, like promotion and distribution, AI has been ready to speed up processes and supply decision-makers with reliable insight. In advertisements, as an example, the automation of market segmentation and campaign management has enabled a lot of well-structured decision-making and fast action. You get valuable insight into your customers, which may assist you to enhance your interactions with them. Marketing automation is amongst the most useful features in a proper customer relations management application.

## 3. Make quicker business decisions supported outputs from cognitive feature technologies

There are several complexities to every marketing decision. You have got to observe and understand client desires and needs and align merchandise to those desires and needs. Likewise, having a decent understanding of fixing client behavior is crucial to creating the most effective selling choices, within the short- and long-term. AI modeling and simulation techniques alter reliable insight into your emptor personas.

4. Avoid mistakes and 'human error,' as long as AI systems are created properly

The margin of human error remains more significant than the margin of AI errors. And chiefly, the supply of AI errors is human error. Investment is required to improve error detection for each sort of mistake to mitigate their impacts. As humans and machines both evolve, the chances of the prevalence of new errors will increase (and of traditional errors decreases), that warrants adequate risk-management efforts.

5. Use insight to predict client preferences and provide them more fabulous, personal experience

Organizations are taking advantage of AI because it allows them to present their customers with personalized promotions, that successively will increase engagement, helps to boost client loyalty and improve sales. Another advantage of AI is that it is ready to identify patterns in customers' browsing habits and shopping behavior, therefore enabling corporations to craft extremely targeted offers to individual customers.

6. Mining immense quantity of data to come up with quality leads and grow your client base

Cloud-based AI applications are quite advanced that they will quickly come upon vital information and relevant findings while processing big data. This feature offers businesses insights into antecedently undiscovered data, which provides them with a higher advantage within the marketplace.

7. Increase revenue by taking note of, and increasing sales opportunities

Pioneers value revenue-generating applications over cost-saving ones. And turning into an AI pioneer is the best edge to produce a probably insurmountable competitive advantage.

8. Grow experience by enabling predictive and risk analysis and giving intelligent recommendation and support

Finally, AI is marvelous in the sense that it will predict outcomes supported by data analysis. For example, it detects patterns in client information that show whether or not the merchandise presently on sale is likely to sell, and also the volume at which they are going to do that. It even can predict the timeline for when such merchandise demand can decrease. This information is fundamental in serving a corporation to purchase the proper stock- and within the right amounts.

The most thrust for the adoption of AI in business was a competitive advantage. After that, the motivation came from:

- An executive-led decision
- A particular company, operational or technical downside
- An internal experiment
- Customer demand
- An immediate answer to an issue

- An effect of another project

## AI Opportunities for Business

It matters not your reason for considering AI; the potential is there for it to change the modus operandi of your business. All it takes to begin is a broad-minded perspective and a temperament to embrace new opportunities whenever and wherever feasible.

Remember, however, that AI is an emerging technology. As such, it is dynamic and quick-paced and should present some unexpected challenges.

## Risks and Limitations of AI in Business

While several business opportunities of AI in the market exist, there also are sure barriers and drawbacks to keep in mind.

One of the significant barriers to implementing AI is data accessibility. Data is regularly archived or is inconsistent, and of poor quality, all of that presents challenges for businesses trying to make value from AI at scale. To beat this, you must have a transparent outline from the point of sourcing the data upon which your AI would depend.

Another key roadblock to AI adoption is the shortage of skills and therefore, the accessibility of technical workers with the expertise and training necessary to effectively deploy and operate AI solutions. Studies suggest seasoned data scientists are sparse as are differently specialized data professionals consummate in machine learning, training smart models, etc.

Cost is another primary consideration of acquiring AI technologies. Businesses that lack in-house skills or are inexperienced with AI typically need to outsource, that is wherein challenges of price and maintenance are come. Thanks to their advanced nature, proper technologies will be high-priced, and you will incur additional costs for repair and in progress maintenance. The processing price for training data models etc. may also be an extra expense.

Software programs require regular upgrading to adapt to the dynamic business setting and just in case of breakdown, introduce a risk of losing code or vital information. Restoring this is typically time-consuming and expensive. However, this risk is not any more significant with AI than with different computer package development. The risks can be managed on the condition that the system is well designed and that you are procuring AI to understand your requirements and options.

Other AI limitations include:

- Implementation times can prove to be extensive, depending on the type of technology you are looking to implement.

- Usability and interoperability with different systems and platforms

If you are deciding whether or not to acquire on AI-driven technology, you must additionally consider:

- Customer privacy
- Potential lack of transparency
- Technological quality

## AI Ethical Issues

Intelligent technologies are enhancing our work and lifestyle. As technology becomes a lot more capable, our world becomes a lot of productive. However, despite the development of our lives, technology giants like IBM, Amazon, or Microsoft, as well as the bright minds like Hawking, believe that now could be the time to speak on matters concerning the future of technology and the way it is impacting the planet. These issues are moral problems but also a lens into the long-run risks. So, what square measure these individuals thus disquieted about?

1. The potential of automation technology to present the rise of job losses

The labor business is generally involved with automation. As we have a tendency to evolve and build other ways of automating jobs, we have a tendency to perhaps additionally introduce a lot of opportunities for folks with advanced roles in the future, moving from the manual and physical work, that characterized the pre-industrial movement, to cognitive labor that is appropriate for the new order of society. With job loss, there is also a need to deploy or retrain staff to retain them in other job posts.

2. Fair redistribution of wealth created by machines

The American financial system relies on compensation for contribution to the economy, typically assessed using an hourly wage. The bulk of corporations are still smitten by hourly work that involves products and services. However, by the use of AI, an organization can drastically level the dependency on human beings, and this suggests that revenues can redistribute to fewer folks. Consequently, people who have possession of AI-driven corporations can amass all the wealth.

3. The result of machine interaction on human behavior and machine interaction

While humans are, to some extent, restricted within the attention and kindness that they will use upon another person, artificial bots will channel nearly unlimited resources into building relationships with humans. It is merely the beginning of an age where we will interact more often with machines as if they were humans.

4. The need to deal with algorithmic bias originating from human bias within the information

Though computer science is capable of speed and capability of processing that is way on the horizon of human capacity, it cannot perpetually be trusted to be honest and impartial. Google and its parent company Alphabet are among the leaders when it involves computer science and Artificial Intelligence. As seen in Google's Photos service, where AI is employed to spot people, objects, and scenes, it could, at times, get it wrong. Like once a camera lost the mark on racial sensitivity, or once a software system accustomed to predict future criminals showed bias against folks of African-American descent. We should not forget that AI systems are created by humans who tend to be biassed and judgmental. Once again, if used right, or if employed by people who attempt for social progress, AI will become a catalyst for positive amendment.

5. The security of AI systems (e.g., autonomous weapons) that may probably cause harm

The increasingly powerful technology becomes, the more it is used for criminal reasons as well as good. Security concerns apply not solely to robots made to replace human troopers or autonomous weapons, but also to AI systems that may cause harm if used maliciously. Because these fights will not be fought on the battlefield solely, cybersecurity has become even more necessary. After all, we are coping with a system that is quicker and highly capable than we are by orders of magnitude.

6. The need to mitigate against unplanned consequences, as smart machines are reliably considered to be taught and develop independently

As we tend to build technology, we want to know the mechanism of reward and aversion, that is employed for humans and animals. For robots, these systems are partly superficial. However, they are turning into more elegant systems. In this scenario, might the machine suffer once it is rewarded with negative input? Some genetic algorithms produce multiple instances of a system quickly; however, only the most successful survive, the remainder are deleted.

While you cannot ignore these risks, it is necessary to keep in mind that advances in AI will- for the most part- produce better business and higher quality of lives for everybody. If enforced responsibly, AI has powerful and useful potential.

# AI In Finance

Followed by AI's massive success in sectors like retail and manufacturing, it is currently ready to transform banking and financial services. The following are several use-cases that banks will take advantage of without delay.

Finance corporations have faith in computers and data scientists to determine the market's future patterns. Commercialism principally depends on the power to predict the long run accurately, and there is nobody better at the duty than machines which may crunch an enormous quantity of data in an exceedingly short period of time. Machines may learn to look at patterns in data history and predict how these patterns would possibly repeat within the future. Aggressive digital transformation is driven by:

• Relentless competition between traditional banks and agile FinTech's and digital-only banks, which are a magnet for customers with progressive service

• The new target automation, big data, analytics, associated innovation adopted in several sectors of the economy together with the finance needs an agile design to support the digital system

• Customers have gotten increasingly digital and tech-savvy especially those of the new generation, particularly below thirty-five years old need to be online and use all advantages of digital mode of services

In the age of very high-frequency commercialism, financial companies are developing AI solutions to enhance their stock trading performance and increase profit. Digital transformation of banks and commercial organizations is essential to leverage the latest technologies and optimize operative and cost efficiencies.

## In-App Banking

Today, nearly all banks have a minimum of one mobile application for carrying out casual banking operations like checking account balance, performing transactions, and ordering new checkbooks, and cards. However, a small number of banks are leveraging AI in their apps to fulfill an outstanding level of customer experience. AI-based chatbots, controlled by natural language processing, can serve banking clients rapidly and proficiently by noting routine inquiries and giving data quickly. Tasks such as opening accounts, transferring money between accounts, paying bills, and process entirely different applications.

## Sales Processes

Chatbots are better at responsive elementary queries of shoppers. They will act as a virtual employee. Chatbots have unique algorithms that assist companies to work together with their customers seamlessly with minimal human intervention.

Sales executives have limitations like operating hours and trade information. Intelligent systems like chatbots do not have any such restrictions. It will answer any queries of shoppers no matter the time as long because the data is offered within the system.

The new system stores an enormous quantity of worth and trading data. By exploiting this reservoir of data, the system will create assessments, for instance, it is going to confirm that current market conditions are the same as the conditions from a month ago and predict however share prices are going to be dynamic minutes down the road. Therefore, shareholders may manage to make better decisions supported by the anticipated market costs.

## Trading

Today, investment firms are looking to data scientists instead of market experts to see the longer-term direction of stocks. The data scientists produce complicated machine learning algorithms that are capable of finding future patterns within the market by being observant of the trends in data history. These algorithms will consume terabytes of data in seconds and might be trained to spot triggers for anomalies happening within the market. Other than that, individual traders may leverage AI to form choices (for them) like when to buy, hold, or sell a stock.

## Compliance Control

Every financial establishment faces a high level of scrutiny. An enormous volume of information is being created each minute by banks. It takes months to spot malpractices like money laundering, market manipulation, foreign regulatory compliance, concealment, etc.

## Risk Analysis

Artificial Intelligence techniques are applied to risk analysis due to its ability to handle uncertainty, incomplete and inexact specifications, vagueness, and qualitative data.

Artificial intelligence and risk management align once there is a necessity in handling and evaluating unstructured data. It is calculable that risk managers of financial establishments focus on analytics and stopping losses in a very proactive manner supported by AI findings, instead of creating time in managing the risks inherent within the operational processes.

AI solutions are ready to fuel financial organizations with trusted and timely information for building competency around their client intelligence and the imminent implementation of their methods.

## Predictive Analytics

As the name suggests predictive analytics, "predicts" a customer's future status. The AI rule predicts what is going to be a customer's status if they will still pay and invest cash just like the manner that they are doing. The machine algorithm can also act as a private financial consultant to a client by providing them a recommendation on how they can improve their status.

## Data Enrichment

Transaction data is often robust for someone- such as a merchant- who spends and receives cash multiple times every day. Transaction data transforms the difficult-to-understand transaction information into easy-to-understand by sorting transactions into categories. It helps customers monitor things like credit rating, budgeting, spending habits, analyzing, and predicting the earnings and spendings of the future.

## Fraud Identification

Both the amount of worldwide transactions and amount in an exceedingly single global transaction is multiplying like a virus; so is the threat of online fraud. The standard online fraud detective algorithm took merely a couple of data points into consideration, whereas AI-based algorithms consider far more data points to spot fraud. Fraud detection is a notable use of AI in financial services. For instance, MasterCard uses Decision Intelligence innovation to examine different data focuses on recognizing fake transactions, improving continuous endorsement precision, and reduce unnecessary transaction delays. Machine Learning algorithms helped the giant payment and technology, MasterCard, to cut back fraudulent activities by fifty percent.

Banks already likely have all of the transaction information tagged because of their storage of bank records from years past. Fraud consultants at the client bank engaged in the machine learning model have got to label the fraudulent transactions and those that are not when the system is being trained. The software system bit by bit improves at discerning between fraud and bonafide banking operations because it is exposed to a lot of tagged transactions.

## Smart Loans

Banks offer loans to their customers, supported by a credit-scoring system. It takes into consideration their banking history, income, tax payments, and more. But, for the customers who have all their money information well-recorded get the upper hand. However, a majority of loan seekers who are underbanked do not have their financial information in bank records.

The new AI-based credit classification system can collect wealth knowledge from the smartphones of underbanked customers to spot their trustworthiness. These different data points can offer new ways for these customers to access credit from the credit banks.

## Wealth Management

Play store and app store offer a variety of wealth management applications that facilitate customers to manage their wealth. These apps leverage a customer's checking account details. Banks have the foresight to steal their customers by introducing an in-app personalized wealth management system. These AI-powered consultants ceaselessly learn from our money activities and supply the most straightforward recommendation to customers, the same as what a relationship manager would do.

A digital revolution is returning within the banking and finance sector with AI. The aim of introducing AI in banking and finance is to deliver pleasant client experiences. It helps customers draw their attention away from understanding numerous banking slang and processes, and instead focus on those things that matter most to them. Specialists predict that the future of AI-based banking mobile app development services is brighter than most people assume.

Financial services organizations use AI-based natural language processing instruments to examine brand opinion from web-based interests and give significant recommendations.

# AI In Medicine

The healthcare sector has been amongst the highest adopters of AI technology. It boils all the way down to the ability of AI to compute numbers fast and learn from historical information, that is essential within the business.

AI can give information-driven clinical decision support (CDS) to doctors and emergency clinic staff preparing for expanded revenue potential. A subset of AI, ML, is intended to distinguish patterns, utilize calculations and information to give automated bits of data to healthcare providers.

For example, Cambio Health Care developed a clinical decision support system for stroke detection that may offer the medical practitioner a warning when there is a patient in danger of getting a stroke. Another such example is Koala Life that may be a company that has developed an AI-powered device that is capable of noticing internal organ diseases, like cardiac arrests.

Artificial Intelligence and ML innovation has been especially helpful in the healthcare industry since it produces tremendous amounts of data to prepare with and performs calculations to spot designs quicker than human experts. Take, for example, Medecision built an algorithm that recognizes eight factors in diabetes patients to decide whether hospitalization is required.

## Clinical Application

The best uses of an AI are augmented intelligence that permits doctors and nurses to perform their best by providing them with timely, data-driven recommendations that they will agree with, reject, or modify supported their personal experience and their judgment of context at that moment in time.

## Keeping Well

One of AI's most prominent potential advantages is to assist individuals to stay healthy so that they do not have to visit a doctor, or not as often. The use of AI and also the Internet of Medical Things (IoMT) in public health applications is already serving to individuals.

Technology applications and applications encourage healthier behavior in people and facilities with the proactive management of a healthy modus vivendi. It puts individuals at the top of their health and well-being.

Also, AI will increase the power for healthcare professionals to better perceive the regular patterns and wishes of the individuals they take care of, and in addition to that understanding, they are then ready to offer better feedback, steerage, and support for staying healthy.

## Detection

AI is already being applied to observe diseases, like cancer, additionally accurately and in their early stages. Consistent with the American Cancer Society, a high proportion of mammograms yield false results, meaning one in a pair of healthy ladies is told that they have cancer. AI is sanctioning review and interpretation of mammograms thirty times quicker with ninety-nine percent accuracy, reducing the requirement for excessive biopsies.

## Diagnosis

Watson for health, by IBM, helps healthcare organizations apply cognitive technology feature to unlock vast amounts of health information and power diagnosis. Watson will review and store much more medical data- each medical journal, symptom, and case study of treatment and response around the world- exponentially quicker than any human.

DeepMind Health, by Google, is functioning in partnership with doctors, researchers, and patients to unravel real-world health issues. The technology combines machine learning and systems neurobiology to create powerful general learning algorithms into neural networks that mimic the human brain.

## Treatment

Beyond scanning health records to assist physicians in establishing inveterately sick people who may also be in danger of succumbing to an adverse episode, AI will facilitate clinicians take a new comprehensive approach for disease management, better coordinate care plans and assist patients in raising, managing, and adjusting to their long-term treatment programs.

Robots have been employed in medicine for over thirty years. They vary from easy laboratory robots to extremely advanced surgical robots that may either aid a person's medico or execute operations by themselves. Not only for surgery, but they are employed in hospitals and labs for repetitive tasks, in rehabilitation, physiatrics, and support of these with long-term conditions.

## Functional Applications

Hospital operations are complicated, extraordinarily different, and deeply interconnected systems — this can be why it is operationally challenging to deliver high utilization of assets, low wait times for patients, and an oversized variety of available slots for patients seeking a rendezvous, all at the same time. The daily operations need many choices being created by the hospital administration staff levels on a regular basis. Sadly, seldom do days go precisely as arranged, and as a result, the battlefront is forced to suppose a static dashboard, half-formed predictions, or gut-feel to create these choices.

## Decision-Making

Improving public healthcare needs the alignment of massive health data with appropriate and timely decisions, and prognostic analytics will support clinical decision-making and actions in addition to prioritizing administrative tasks.

Using pattern recognition to spot patients in danger of developing a condition- or seeing it deteriorate thanks to lifestyle, environmental, genomic, or different factors- is another space where AI is setting out to take hold in medicine. Many data analytics systems concentrate on "descriptive analytics" that answer questions like "what happened." AI permits the analytics to maneuver more toward "prescriptive analytics" that makes recommendations regarding "what ought to happen." The intent is to leverage the information and continuous machine learning to assist the battlefront systematically create the most privy choices across all sorts of circumstances.

Patient care and operations are two totally different, everyday samples of ways in which AI will disrupt the healthcare business. There is an infinite number of additional examples, and nevertheless, hopefully, these demonstrate the very fact that AI harnesses unimaginable amounts of data to boost the expertise in both large and smaller ways.

## Research

The path from the laboratory to the patient may be a long and expensive one. Consistent with a Golden State medical specialty analysis Association, it takes about twelve years for a drug to travel from the research laboratory to the patient. A measly five in five thousand of the medication that begins presymptomatic testing ever reach human experimentation and only 1 of those five is ever approved for human usage. What is more, on average, it will cost an organization US $359 million to develop a brand new drug from the laboratory to the patient.

Drug research is among the newer applications for AI in healthcare. By leading the latest advances in AI to shape the drug discovery and drug repurposing processes, there is the potential to shred both the cost and time to market considerably.

# Training

AI permits those in training to travel through realistic simulations that straightforward computer-driven algorithms cannot. The arrival of natural language and therefore the ability of AI computers to draw instantly on an oversized database of eventualities, means that the response to queries, decisions, or recommendations from a trainee will pose a more significant challenge that a person. Therefore, the training program will learn from previous responses from the student, which means that the problems are often regularly adjusted to satisfy their learning desires. And training is often done anywhere; with the ability of AI embedded in a smartphone, fast catch up sessions, after a problematic case during a clinic or in motion, are possible.

Optimization models that learn and adapt will facilitate the improvement of the productive capability of the various valuable assets in a health system. These assets include operation theaters, patients beds, and imaging instruments, to name a few. AI will dictate the fate of medicine as a result of its potential to enhance patient care, bring on higher outcomes, and enhance the expertise, whereas utilizing better the existing resources. The resources at hand help doctors, schedule groups, facility managers, and ultimately even insurance corporations. As additional AI-based solutions are adopted and placed into play, expect an entirely new world of opportunities to open up, which will remodel healthcare for the better.

# Conclusion

Thank you for making it through to the end of *ARTIFICIAL INTELLIGENCE AND MACHINE LEARNING: AI Superpowers and Human + Machine A Visionary Revolution in Finance, Medicine and Business. Find Out 10 Most Influent People of the Era With A Modern Approach*. I hope that it was informational and was able to provide you with the basic knowledge you need to understand the concepts of Artificial Intelligence and machine learning. By finishing this book, you will be able to possess the mastery that you seek in understanding the role of artificial intelligence in influencing human behaviors in different facets of life.

We have gone through the definition, goals, and types of artificial intelligence and machine learning. This book has offered easy-to-use but very powerful and effective definition of concepts that are crucial in understanding artificial intelligence. It provides a great overview of how the world is gradually adapting to the technological changes with the aid of artificial intelligence and machine learning. You are now familiar with the relationship between AI and machine learning, as well as the possible differences. You have also learned that almost every aspect of our careers are gradually embracing AI for efficiency.

You are now aware of the key concepts of AI and machine learning, and how they work. The next thing you would want to do is to decide to invest in the field due to the vast opportunities available. With the knowledge of superpowers in AI and machine learning development, you can further learn the more opportunities that exist in such technology.

Finally, if you found this book useful in any way, a review on Amazon is always appreciated!